# Writing a Musical

Richard Andrews has to date worked on twenty-two West End shows, of which eighteen were new pieces. These have ranged from the hugely successful *Jesus Christ Superstar* and *Me and My Girl* to the spectacularly unsuccessful *Barnado* and *Jukebox* with both ends of the spectrum providing a useful learning experience. During this time his work has covered all aspects of theatre production, from stage manager through to producer. In 1988 Richard Andrews co-founded FACADE, an organization which creates, promotes and produces new works in musical theatre.

# Writing a Musical

RICHARD ANDREWS

ROBERT HALE · LONDON

ISBN 0 7090 5913 2

Robert Hale Limited
Clerkenwell House
Clerkenwell Green
London EC1R 0HT

2  4  6  8  10  9  7  5  3  1

Photoset in North Wales by
Derek Doyle & Associates, Mold, Flintshire.
Printed in Great Britain by
St Edmundsbury Press Ltd, Bury St Edmunds, Suffolk.
Bound by WBC Book Manufacturers Limited,
Bridgend, Mid-Glamorgan.

To Mary Stewart-David
– for inspiration and exasperation

# Contents

# Acknowledgements

'I Don't Know How To Love Him', © Copyright MCA Music Limited.

'I Feel Pretty'. Music by Leonard Bernstein. Lyrics by Stephen Sondheim © Copyright 1957 (renewed) by Leonard Bernstein and Stephen Sondheim. Jalni Publications Incorporated/Boosey & Hawkes Incorporated, USA & Canadian publisher. G Schirmer Incorporated, worldwide print rights & publisher for the rest of the world. G Schirmer Limited/Campbell Connelly & Company Limited, 8/9 Frith Street, London W1V 5TZ. Used by permission of Music Sales Limited. All Rights Reserved. International Copyright Secured.

'Guess Who I Saw Today?' Words & Music by Murray Grand & Elisse Boyd © Copyright 1952 Santly-Joy Incorporated, USA. Campbell Connelly & Company Limited, 8/9 Frith Street, London W1V 5TZ. Used by permission of Music Sales Limited. All Rights Reserved. International Copyright Secured.

'Tell Me On A Sunday'. Music by Andrew Lloyd Webber. Lyrics by Don Black. Music © Copyright 1979 The Really Useful Group Limited. Text © Copyright 1979 Dick James Music Limited. Used by permission of Music Sales Limited. All Rights Reserved. International Copyright Secured.

'Wishing You Were Somehow Here Again' & 'Why Have You Brought Me Here?'/'Raoul, I've Been There' from *The Phantom of the Opera*. Music: Andrew Lloyd Webber. Lyrics: Charles Hart. Additional Lyrics: Richard Stilgoe. © Copyright 1986 The Really Useful Group Limited, London. All Rights Reserved. International Copyright Secured.

# Figures

# Introduction

Charles Strange said: 'Man has three basic drives: food, sex and criticizing other people's musicals'. He may have got the order wrong.

What is it about musicals? They have the power to touch more people than any other art form. They are capable of soaring to the greatest heights of emotion when they work, and the lowest depths of bathos when they don't.

Why is it that whenever I have actually been moved to tears in the theatre, it has always been at a musical? Each time I have seen *Man of La Mancha*, a perceptible sniff echoed round the auditorium when the hero died. Why is it that on other occasions, even though my only reaction was to gasp at the ineptitude of the writing, there were people with tears streaming down their cheeks when the lights came up?

Is it the immediacy of the live performance – real reality in the age of the virtual? Could it be that the ability to almost reach out and touch the characters draws an audience further into the story, and creates a stronger bond? Why do films of stage musicals almost always get it so wrong? Why does the translation to a different medium so often result in losing the very thing that made the original so special?

Why are musicals so hard to get right? History is littered not only with talented writers from other fields who have tried and failed, but also with masters of the craft who suddenly come a cropper. Don Black, arguably this country's most successful lyricist ever, also gave us *Bar Mitzvah Boy* and *Budgie*. Why do they arouse such passion and blind faith in their creators? How could they promote *Liza of Lambeth* with a radio advertisement featuring the lyric:

LIZA, OH LIZA, YOU'RE AS LONDON AS THE RAILINGS
AND ALTHOUGH YOU'VE GOT YOUR FAILINGS
YOU ARE STRAIGHT AS NELSON'S COLUMN?

Why do I and so many other people get involved in musicals? You have to be mad to want to take part in a business where the odds are stacked so high against success, and you leave yourself so open to ridicule. Working in the theatre is one thing (you can perhaps do theatre and stay in control), but once you've tried musicals, it's too late – there's no way back. Plays are just not satisfying enough.

Why is it that, even when they're bad, musicals are so memorable? I can look through the programmes of the hundreds of evenings I have spent in the theatre, and, while some of the plays (even with great names in them) I can barely recall, the musicals come instantly to mind. Why is it that even super-flops find a place in our hearts? *Which Witch* literally had all hell breaking loose as spirits flew out over the audience. *Leonardo* featured an amputee on a trolley who gamely joined in the choreography (and the audience laughed so much the seats shook). *Fields of Ambrosia* ended with the leading man (also the writer) in the electric chair, uttering the immortal line 'Fry me while I'm hot'.

At the midweek matinee (the only midweek matinee) of *Thomas and the King* just the stalls were open, and the usherette bade us: 'Sit where you like, but do try to huddle together down the front'. Then there was Cameron Mackintosh's first West End production – *Anything Goes* – which opened on Thursday and closed on Saturday. The preview of Andrew Lloyd Webber and Alan Ayckbourn's original production of *Jeeves*; afterwards I dared not go round to see my friends in it, because I couldn't think of anything to say that was either helpful or encouraging – even the old fence-sitting standby 'You did it again!'

seemed inadequate. Why do I still treasure memories such as these? Perhaps because, having worked on one of the most vilified shows of all time (*Barnardo*), I know what people go through.

What is it that all successes share? The ability to touch our emotions, to involve us in the events that are unfolding, to care about the characters we are watching, or to amuse and stimulate us? What is it that all flops share? A fundamental lack of understanding of how a musical works, of what is acceptable to an audience – how far their suspension of disbelief can be strained before it snaps – or of the nature of drama *per se*?

The answers to these and many other questions will not be found in this book. If all the answers were known (by me or anybody else), we would all be rich, and there would be no flops.

## Why write this book?

When we started FACADE, we encouraged people to send us their musicals, because we thought that one script in a hundred might be produceable. It rapidly became apparent that one in a thousand (maybe ten thousand) might be nearer the mark. The reason seemed to be that so many writers lacked basic knowledge, and the problem was that there was nowhere for them to acquire it. In an effort to help writers, and make our lives both more bearable and productive, we decided to find a way to solve the problem.

On an irregular basis, we started running a two-day introductory course called 'Making A Musical'. Its aim was to provide basic information, and to make writers and composers more aware of what needs to be taken into consideration when creating a musical. It also offered them the opportunity to ask questions and discuss their current projects. As the years have gone by, we have continually striven to refresh and extend the scope of the course. Our participants have ranged in expertise from sixth-formers about to make their first attempt, to BBC producer Alfred Bradley, keen as ever to conquer new fields.

This book explores the themes and ideas of the course at great length, and in the form of a reference work that you can keep to hand to help guide you through the creative process. It also includes a resources section – listing books, journals, useful organizations, courses, suppliers and web sites that may be of further assistance on that journey – and a glossary where you can look up any terms you don't know.

Writing a musical is like a plate-spinning act. You have to keep a balance in so many things, with plot development, character development, drama, comedy, song, speech, variety of content all going at the same time. I aim at least to ensure that you start off with a decent set of sticks and plates, and to help you to develop that sixth sense which tells you the one at the end is about to fall.

Of course, this book is entirely subjective. It is the sum of my experience after working in all manner of guises on over twenty West End shows, ranging from the hugely successful to the spectacularly unsuccessful. In some cases my associates already had the money and the drain, and I simply provided the shovel. In others I arrived like Superman to save them from themselves in the nick of time. This has enabled me to form some very definite opinions, which I share with you in these pages. A book like this can't teach you to be creative, or turn you into a great writer, but it can encourage you to think in more productive ways, and help you to make the most of your writing ability. I don't claim to know all the answers, but I do know some of the questions – which puts me ahead of most people.

## A complete history of the musical in less than a page

Some people consider that the first musical was *The Beggar's Opera* in 1728. If so, it didn't catch on, because there wasn't another musical for two hundred years. Others think that musicals are descended from nineteenth-century light opera – Gilbert and Sullivan, Offenbach, Lehar, Strauss. I'm not one of them.

I think that the musical is the art form of the twentieth century. It comes from the spectacular revues of Florenz Ziegfeld, the Music Box and others in America, and C.B. Cochrane, Herbert Farjeon and others here during the first two or three decades of the century. The writers who became most important in the early musicals – Kern, Porter, Berlin, the Gershwins, Rodgers and Hart and Hammerstein – all learnt their trade by contributing songs and sketches to revues. They grew more ambitious and the public grew with them. Although there were others in the 1920s (many of them little more than themed revues), I think the first important musical was *Showboat* in 1927. The next milestone was *Porgy and Bess* in 1935.

The post-war years were the time that the American musical came to its peak, with *Oklahoma!*, *South Pacific* and *My Fair Lady*, and drew to a close with *The Sound of Music*. There was a revolution in 1966 with *Hair*, which launched the rock musical, followed by *Jesus Christ Superstar* as the British milestone in 1972.

The eighties and nineties belong to Andrew Lloyd Webber, with *Cats* and *The Phantom of the Opera*, and Boublil and Schonberg, with *Les Miserables* and *Miss Saigon*, although of course everyone defers to Sondheim as the world's greatest talent in creating musicals. If Shakespeare were alive today, I think he would be Stephen Sondheim. Perhaps the most important thing for prospective writers of musicals to remember is that – as he says 'Musicals aren't written, they're rewritten'.

# 1   The Basic Concept

Thomas Alva Edison said: 'Genius is one per cent inspiration and ninety-nine per cent perspiration', and this is particularly true of musicals. More than in any other creative endeavour, the spark of an idea for a musical can come in a moment, but its execution will usually take years – and both are equally important to a successful outcome.

## What is meant by Concept?

When people hear you are writing a musical, the first question is always: 'What's it about?' Usually, the answer is, 'It's about two-and-three-quarter hours, but we're working on the second act', but you should have a better answer ready than that. You should tell them The Concept. The concept defines in a sentence or two what the idea is, and how it is to be treated. It should encapsulate the artistic and commercial potential. Whatever its subject matter, a musical, if it is to be successful, must be the story of a sympathetic character who overcomes a reversal of fortune, and it must achieve a satisfactory conclusion.

Lionel Bart has said, 'If you can't sell an idea in a sentence, don't waste your time writing it'. If you are going to spend two years writing a show (and that's the usual development time) you have to make sure you've got a viable idea that you can communicate effectively to a potential producer – and that he in turn can communicate to potential investors, and finally to a potential audience. So you must be able to say something like:

> *Miss Saigon* is the story of *Madam Butterfly* set in the Vietnam war.

You should also be able to define the treatment as well as the subject matter. If, for instance, it's a musical version of *The Satanic Verses*:

> Will it be a one-man show, or have a cast of fifty?
> Will it use traditional Middle-Eastern music, or sound like Sondheim?
> Will it be a conventional book musical, or through-written?

The concept could be:

> A musical version of *The Satanic Verses*, with a cast of ten, employing traditional Middle-Eastern music, in a through-written form.

One sentence tells you all you need to know.

The concept for an original story is always: The story of (*someone*) who (*does something*) which is told (*in some way*). For an adaptation (since the story will already be known), it is always: The story of (*source work*) told in (*a unique way*).

More important than being able to communicate your idea to other people, is to be able to define it for yourself and your collaborators. It is so easy to get side-tracked; you can fall in love with a particular character, or an idea for a scene or number, and the show can veer off in a wholly irrelevant direction. You must continually ask yourself: what is it about? How does this particular scene or song further that concept?

The fully developed concept should have:

> *A hero* (of either gender) with whom the audience can identify, through whom they can experience emotion, whose motivation drives the plot.

A *plot*, whose obstacles or reversals of fortune require the hero to exhibit some sort of physical or emotional courage and moral purpose, resulting in spiritual growth.

A *theme*, drawn from the plot, which is a timeless universal statement about the human condition.

*Originality* in the development of the story and the method employed in its telling.

Remember, above all, that the heart of any story is conflict.

## But first: the Idea

In order to have a Concept, you first need the Idea – so let us consider where it may come from. Most successful musicals have been adaptations from other media: books, plays, films, or even comic strips. Why? Perhaps because original musicals are so difficult to write. They aren't just three times more difficult than a play (because they have book, music and lyrics), they are more like factorial three (or twenty-seven) times more difficult to write. Think how many flops established writers have had. Even Rodgers and Hammerstein's original works (*Allegro* and *Me and Juliet*) were failures; it's very difficult to get right.

Adapting existing material does give you an overall framework, which concentrates the different minds and gives a shape that works dramatically in one medium at least. As Mark Steyn says: 'With adaptation, composer, lyricist and librettist at least know the destination and can concentrate their skills on figuring out how to get there'. Adaptation worked for Euripides and Shakespeare, whose plays have subsequently themselves been adapted for operas and musicals. Alan Jay Lerner said that adapting an existing story was a big enough creative challenge for anyone.

Adaptation also provides a useful marketing tool. Arousing the curiosity of your potential audience in what you have done with a story they know may be easier than interesting it in a totally unknown quantity.

When selecting your subject, you must first ask yourself why make a musical out of this story? What can it add? Musicalizing books and films allows you to explore the story in a different medium. Musicalizing plays, on the other hand, often detracts from their power, rather than adding to it. Your vision must enhance the source material. It must be a sympathetic amplification of the original, not something that is simply grafted on; there is no inherent need for a musical version of any existing work. Arthur Laurens wrote 'Many people object to musicals on the ground that they are merely reworking of old and familiar material. The trouble, rather, is that the material is *not* reworked: it is merely edited, and songs are dropped in.'

You must have an original idea, not a second-hand one. It should be fresh and have something new to say, otherwise there is no point in doing it. I have read four different versions of *Trilby* (who knows how many others there are), and only one brought something new to the telling of the story. Don't be the ninety-ninth person to write 'Sherlock Holmes: The Musical'. (Sorry, I was forgetting Leslie Bricusse – don't be the one hundredth.)

Whatever your initial idea, though – be it an original story or an adaptation of existing material – its development (how you choose to tell that story) is just as important in getting the full value from it. The show must have a point of view, and you must find the right voice for the idea to express itself. For example, *Moby Dick – A Whale of a Tale* by Robert Longdon and Hereward Kaye has a wonderful premise: Herman Melville's dark story performed as an end-of-term musical at a girls' school. The incongruity of tiny girl dancers playing Starbuck and Queequeg was wonderfully theatrical. Sadly, though, the enterprise was sunk by the way it was developed, with a reliance on lavatorial humour, and finally by its crude execution. To be successful, your idea must have what they call in business a USP (Unique Selling Point), but it must be a creative one, expressed in the way you tell the story, rather than a physical one that is expressed through the set or through production tricks, like a helicopter, boat or machine room.

Let's consider how a few writers have used their subject

as inspiration for its development into musical theatre. *The Mystery of Edwin Drood*, an adaptation of Dickens' last unfinished novel, uses the form of a Victorian Music Hall, with the audience voting on 'whodunnit' at the end. *City of Angels*, is the story of a detective-story writer adapting his work for the screen. The scenes from the film are staged in black and white, with the action 'rewound' and replayed in different versions; the author even duets with his creation. *The Baker's Wife* is the tale of a spring-and-autumn marriage in a Provence village. The baker actually makes bread while singing 'Plain and Simple', using it to illustrate his philosophy. *Man of La Mancha* employs Cervantes' imprisonment by the Inquisition as a framework for telling the story of Don Quixote. *Barnum*, with its circus ring setting uses minimal resources to give the illusion of the greatest show on earth. Many seemingly unlikely concepts have been successful. Imagine trying to explain to someone for the first time the idea of *Cats*, *Pippin* or even *Sweeney Todd*.

Whatever the story, the theme must relate to today, regardless of where or when it is actually set. *Windy City*, the musical based on *The Front Page*, is on the surface a 1930s farcical comedy about newspaper men, but its theme is the sacrifice of the individual through political corruption. To be successful, though you must start with the story and let the theme develop out of it – not the other way round. *Martin Guerre* diminishes the original subject by imposing a framework of religious persecution; and the flood of 'message' plays in the 1970s put a whole generation off theatre-going. Overt moralizing is not suitable for the musical theatre.


## Where does the story start?

In adapting material you may make radical changes for the musical form. It can be said that a musical that is totally faithful to its source probably won't be a good musical. The source material needs to be rediscovered in musical terms.

21

Music allows you to compress time. It transmits feelings and ideas instantaneously, creating an atmosphere and spirit that it would take many words to create. You can convey in a musical number what takes an entire scene of dialogue. In print, *Green Grow The Lilacs* runs to 162 pages, while its musical adaptation *Oklahoma!* takes just 77. Alternatively, music can give you the space to make the most of a dramatic or emotional moment, to realize its full value in a way that, in mere dialogue, could seem overwritten.

You might start the story earlier than the source material, to sketch in the characters' background. *My Fair Lady* introduces the character of Doolittle (via 'With a Little Bit Of Luck') in a new scene at a point in the story well before he makes his appearance in Pygmalion. Alternatively, you may create an opening number that can telescope the first few scenes of the original and cut straight to the meat of the story. In *Oliver!*, Lionel Bart has the courage to plunge into the story at the point we know best, with 'Food, Glorious Food'. There may be characters who are no more than mentioned in the original, whom you could introduce to flesh out the story for the stage. Thus, in *Oklahoma!*, Will Parker becomes Ado Annie's opposite number in a whole new sub-plot, which also enhances her character. Any adaptation will be a process of selection and development. As Dr Samuel Johnson may have remarked: 'Sir, in the making of musical adaptations, no man is on oath'.

*Oliver!* is probably one of the best examples of a show that maintains the feel of the original, while selecting one strong storyline and a couple of sub-plots from a massive source. In contrast, the first act of *Les Miserables* is like an American television mini series, because it tries to cover too much ground; it's all births and deaths of people who aren't seen enough to become fully developed characters. *Les Miserables* might work much better if the whole show was set in Paris at the time of the uprising, with one brief flashback of how Valjean and Javert came to be in conflict with each other, and another of how Cosette became Valjean's ward. It would bring the whole thing down to manageable proportions.

At the opposite end of the scale, shows like *South Pacific*,

*Fiddler on the Roof* and *Cabaret* interweave different short stories into one cohesive plot. That idea doesn't always work, though. Look at the original version of *Jeeves*. It tried to cram too many characters and storylines into one show, and, with a book written by Alan Ayckbourn, it was Andrew Lloyd Webber's only flop. In *South Pacific* Rodgers and Hammerstein not only took three separate stories – Nellie Forbush/Emile de Beck; Lt Cable/Liat/Bloody Mary; and Luther Billis – but they even enhanced these characters by borrowing details from other stories (for example, the theme of Emile's children by an oriental wife).

Adapting a play or film may seem easier than a book, since someone else has already extracted the drama. Stephen Sondheim's *Passion* is based on a film of a book. The fact is that no two people adapting or telling the same story would end up with the same material. Always go back to the original source. Your storytelling must have a point of view about the events which you portray that relates to today's audience; what someone else, at some other time, may have considered as the important elements may not be what you feel is important now. Changing times mean changing perceptions. A straight revival of *Me and my Girl, Anything Goes* or *Girl Crazy* would probably not have worked, but reinvented, with new numbers and a revised book (and even a new name: *Girl Crazy* became *Crazy for You*), they were huge successes again. It does depend on the skills of the re-interpreters, though; it didn't work for *High Society*, or *Some Like It Hot*.

## The best collaborator ...

If you do decide to adapt an existing work, you must consider the implications of copyright. When somebody creates something, they have a right to some financial reward from its exploitation, and this goes on until seventy years after their death. Copyright is a complex issue, and *The Writers' and Artists' Yearbook* has a section that covers it well. But the basic point is, if the writer is still alive (or hasn't been dead long enough) you will need his or her agreement (or that of his or her legatee) to adapt a work. Real people can't be copyrighted, but their creations – that is their performing *personae* (such as Charlie Chaplin's 'little tramp') – can.

Some people say that if you have an idea, you shouldn't worry about the rights but just go ahead, write, and show the result to the original author afterwards. Take heed! It's nice to think that he or she will be flattered and charmed by your work – but it's far more likely that he or she will either hate musicals, or be working on an alternative project with someone else, and so will refuse permission for your adaptation to be performed.

Don't waste two years of your life by taking this chance. Find out, via the publisher, who the copyright agent is, and check. The author may be quite happy for you to go ahead, and may even want to be involved. Alternatively, he or she may expect you to buy an option for a specific period while you work on it. With one idea we had, the author wanted £5000 for a two-year option, with no guarantee that he would allow it to be performed when it was written; we had to shelve the idea. We organized a workshop for a producer who had funded a creative process, which had lasted through five years and two book writers. In the end, the author's estate didn't like the adaptation and wouldn't allow it to be performed. This is just one reason why many people believe that the best collaborator is one who is long dead.

There are those who say that writing something, even if it can't be performed, is a valuable experience, and you should be happy with that. Do you really want to put yourself through the effort and heartache of writing a musical when you can never have the satisfaction of seeing it come to fruition? There is enough disappointment in this business as it is. Don't beg for more; always write with the aim of production in mind.

## Sympathetic characters

Whatever your story, original or adaptation, the characters and situations must be sympathetic. Take *The Phantom of the Opera*. The source material is a conventional horror story, and the Phantom is the villain. In the musical he is presented sympathetically. You want him to get the girl (and not just because he's played by Michael Crawford). Francis Ford Coppola used a similar technique in his film of Dracula. You have to get the audience rooting for the characters, and hoping that their story will work out right in the end. They must want to cheer the hero, hiss the villain, and swoon over the heroine, even if only metaphorically. Unsympathetic characters in an unattractive situation will only provoke disinterest.

In the past *Jack the Ripper* flopped at the box office, even though it worked as a show. So did *Flowers for Algernon* (in spite of having Michael Crawford in it), because people did not empathize with the leading characters. When *Mack and Mabel* finally opened in London, the general consensus was that – despite the wonderful score and an attempt at a revised 'upbeat' ending – it still didn't work. The characters and their story were not sympathetic. Also, like *Jack the Ripper*, it broke the rule that leading characters must be morally sound. That is why there has so far been no successful musical about Raffles, the 'gentleman' burglar who stole from his friends.

These considerations are all part of the commercial potential of the idea. You must ask yourself why should anyone want to pay the money, and make the effort of coming to see this? Will they feel sufficiently satisfied by the outcome to encourage someone else to do the same?

That doesn't mean, though, that musicals have to be trite, or can't tackle serious subjects. As Joseph Stein says, 'There are no limitations to the subject of a musical, any more than a play or novel.' But the material does have to be presented in a way that is suited to the medium. You can't beat people over the head with an iron bar in a musical; you must use some ingenuity and subtlety. Take, for instance, the songs 'You've Got To Be Carefully

Taught' in *South Pacific*, or 'If You Could See Her' in *Cabaret*, which are about racism. Be warned by 'Bui-Doi', the second-act opening number in *Miss Saigon*, with its crude attempt to manipulate the emotions of the audience by using film of actual Vietnamese children.


## What doesn't work

Certain kinds of material have so far been proved unsuitable for musical adaptation. They are thrillers, farce and fantasy/science-fiction.

Thrillers and farce are plot-driven, rather than character-driven. Thriller plots are too complex, and the maintenance of suspense makes them unsuitable for musical interpolation. There have been various attempts – most recently with *The Case of the Dead Flamingo Dancer* and Ruth Rendell's *Judgement in Stone*, neither of which succeeded. The one that came closest to success was *Something's Afoot*, which was a spoof Agatha Christie story, with an ever-diminishing group trapped in a large country house – and therefore a comedy rather than a real thriller.

Similarly in farce, there is a problem of interrupting the pace of the action. In addition, there is a degree of introspection inherent in musicals that is not really consistent with the principles of farce. Some years ago Ray Cooney tried unsuccessfully to musicalize *Not Now Darling*. The exception was *A Funny Thing Happened on the Way to the Forum*. This was subject to much reworking during production, and eventually they found that the solution was to use the numbers as rests from the action.

With science fiction or fantasy, the problem is that the heightened reality of the musical cannot start from a premise that is itself founded in unreality. There have been few professional attempts to produce shows in this area, but *Time* should be a firm enough warning for anyone. Once again there is an exception, and it is a big one: *Cats*.

Television adaptations are generally too small an idea

for the stage. What fills half an hour or an hour of screen time is lost when a whole evening on the stage is devoted to it, as *Budgie* and *Bar Mitzvah Boy* demonstrate. In addition, the premise of *Budgie* (set in the strip clubs of 1960s Soho) had not stood the test of time; what was acceptable when first written had, by the time of the musical twenty years later, become an unsympathetic character in a sordid story.

In a 'quest' show, the hero is involved in some sort of journey. He continually meets new characters (who almost inevitably have a number each), and there is a high risk that they will appear more interesting than the hero, and therefore swamp him. *The Hunting of the Snark* was an example of this mistake (and many others). The episodic nature of such stories, lacking highs and lows (since no one section is more important than any other), means that they lack a proper structure. Like a sliced loaf, they have no satisfying shape and just go on until they stop. I once worked on a musical of *The Water Babies*, which was presented twice daily. There wasn't a long enough break between shows, so it was necessary to shorten the first performance. One episode – scene, character and song – was simply cut; character A directed the hero to character C instead of character B. It made perfect sense, and nobody noticed the join (although they missed a great number sung by a walrus on roller skates, long before *Starlight Express* was thought of).

Musical biographies, though writers seem to find them tempting, are similarly very difficult. Real people never lead lives that have a satisfying dramatic shape. This is most recently and ably demonstrated by *Jolson*. In Act I, he's boorish and rows with his first wife and his producer. In Act II, he's boorish and rows with his second wife and his agent. Real lives tend to peak well before the end and then go downhill, so it's difficult to find the right conclusion (and, anyway, where do you put the interval?). Most importantly, it is usually impossible to demonstrate on the stage the particular characteristic or quality that made the subject unique. There's nothing more boring for an audience than the cast banging on about how extraordinary a particular character is, when there hasn't been any evidence of it.

Backstage musicals are equally popular with writers, and there is almost always one as a finalist in the Vivian Ellis Prize for new writers. The problem is that they need to be about universal themes that transcend what Stanley Lebowsky referred to as 'the business we call show'. It comes as a huge surprise to most people working in the theatre that, in the GP's (general public's) opinion, they are lazy, whinging, self-centred egotists! To spark their interest, audiences have to be given something they can really relate to.

Compilation shows are not musicals; they are musical entertainments (some more entertaining than others). Often they are just slapdash, cheap attempts to cash in on a songwriter's reputation. *Side by Side by Sondheim* had a unique format – as its crop of failed emulators have conclusively proved. The addition of scraps of biographical material to a collection of songs doesn't make a musical. The only show of this kind which could possibly be called a musical is the original *Elvis* by Jack Good and Ray Cooney; its particular combination of writing, staging and spectacle did make a real theatrical experience that distinguished it from a few singers going through a list of numbers, like *Ain't Misbehavin'*. The other kind of compilation show is a loose story woven around songs of a particular period or theme like *Five Guys Named Moe*.

## Dramatic unities

Musical theatre should not obey the unities of Time, Place and Action promulgated as the basis of drama by Aristotle. Music enables you to telescope time and place in a manner which in a straight play would be unacceptable. The 'Opening Doors' sequence in *Merrily We Roll Along* covers a two-year period during which the principal characters attempt to get their careers started. It's a masterpiece of construction that is almost a whole show in itself.

Musicals demand a fast pace, short scenes and multiple locations – there can be no such thing as a 'box-set' musical. In this, they have more in common with television plays than stage plays. I read a script that was set entirely in the reception area of a solicitors' office; you could argue that all human life was there, but it was just passing through! It is never credible for people to play private scenes in public places. When it gets interesting, the action moves behind closed doors, and the audience needs to move with it.

Many box-set plays have been opened out into musicals, *Windy City* for instance. It has even been done to a story as claustrophobic as *On the Twentieth Century*, which was set entirely on a train. Consider in Figure 1 how *My Fair Lady* compares with the original *Pygmalion*.

### Figure 1   *Pygmalion* and *My Fair Lady*: Time and Place Comparison

| *Pygmalion* | *My Fair Lady* | |
| --- | --- | --- |
| | **Act I**: | |
| **Act I**: Outside Covent Garden | **Scene 1**: | Outside Covent Garden |
| | **Scene 2**: | Tenement in Tottenham Court Road (*Immediately following*) |
| **Act II**: Higgins' laboratory (*Next day*) | **Scene 3**: | Higgins' study (*Next morning*) |
| | **Scene 4**: | Tenement in Tottenham Court Road (*Three Days Later*) |
| | **Scene 5**: | Higgins' study (*Later that day*) |
| **Act III**: Mrs Higgins 'At Home' | **Scene 6**: | Ascot, near the race meeting (*A July afternoon*) |
| | **Scene 7**: | Ascot, inside a club tent (*Immediately following*) |

|  | **Scene 8**: | Outside Higgins' house |
|---|---|---|
|  |  | (*Later that afternoon*) |
|  | **Scene 9**: | Higgins' study |
|  |  | (*Six weeks later*) |
|  | **Scene 10**: | The Embassy Ballroom |

**Act II**:

| **Act IV**: Higgins' laboratory | **Scene 1**: | Higgins' study |
|---|---|---|
|  |  | (*3 a.m. next morning*) |
|  | **Scene 2**: | Outside Higgins' house |
|  |  | (*Immediately following*) |
|  | **Scene 3**: | Covent Garden Market |
|  | **Scene 4**: | Higgins' upstairs hall |

| **Act V**: Mrs Higgins' drawing-room | **Scene 5**: | Mrs Higgins' conservatory |
|---|---|---|
|  | **Scene 6**: | Outside Higgins' house |
|  | **Scene 7**: | Higgins' study |
|  |  | (*Immediately following*) |

---

## Size isn't everything

Abandoning Aristotle's unities does not necessarily mean that musicals demand casts of thousands and huge sets. Shakespeare worked in a multiple-scene format with no scenery at all, and I have personally worked on a production of *Henry IV* Parts I/II and *Henry V* with a cast of twelve, a standing set, two benches, a table and a chair.

Old-fashioned shows usually had a large chorus of singers and dancers, generally referred to as 'jolly villagers'. For no good reason they wafted on to the stage when a big number was about to happen, and then wafted off again afterwards. They weren't real characters, and they didn't have any genuine contribution to make to the story; they just provided sound and colour (as in most operas). It is disturbing that they seem to be making a comeback. For instance, both *Aspects of Love* and *Sunset Boulevard* seem to be small shows trying to fight their way out of big ones; their stories revolve around five characters, but involve casts of twenty-five. Perhaps it is one of the disadvantages of directors who work in both opera and musical theatre: they bring bad habits with them. You should not follow suit.

Ten years ago there was a rash of 'event' shows, like *Time*, *Mutiny* and *Metropolis*, where the main creative thrust appeared to come from the designer, rather than the author. We then took a step back from the implied equation: Spectacle + Volume = Success – largely because it didn't. It is disturbing that this principal is being reasserted by turning previously small-scale works into 'mega-musicals': inflating them by adding an unnecessary chorus and huge sets. Recent West End productions of *Joseph*, *Oliver!* and *Grease* were all similarly 'over-produced', and artistically less successful than previous productions staged with much smaller resources. Nevertheless, they have been very successful financially.

## Artistic conventions

When you write, you set your own artistic conventions. You can use contemporary music and language for a period subject, if you want to. When Richard Rodgers wrote *The King and I*, he was asked if he had written Siamese music. He replied, 'No, I've written Jewish music, just the same as I always do.' Boublil and Schonberg have a similar philosophy with *Miss Saigon* – it's actually hard to tell if a number comes from that or *Les Miserables*. But don't choose a convention that is obviously unsympathetic to the subject: a punk version of *Pride and Prejudice*, for instance. Above all, once you have established your convention, you must work within its rules. Audiences will generally accept anything except a change of mind halfway through.

It has been said that the quintessential British musical is set in a stately home in Sussex where some undesirable person (a member of the working class or, even worse, an American) is educated, under protest, by an impoverished member of the upper class – the whole usually set in motion by the family solicitor at the reading of a will. (I refer you to *Me and My Girl, The Amazons* and *Peg*.) Very few major musicals have been located in a contemporary setting. In the last thirty years, only *Hair, Sweet Charity, Promises, Promises, Company, La Cage aux Folles, They're Playing Our Song, Chess* and *A Chorus Line* have been successful – and none of these are recent. It may, again, be because the heightened reality of the musical form conflicts with an expectation of modern naturalism (though whether bursting into song came any more naturally to Victorians than it does to us is debatable). Perhaps a truly modern musical would attract a new generation to musical theatre.

When you are first starting out, don't try to redefine the musical form. You will be much more likely to be able to do that successfully with your next show. Firstly you will have more experience, and, secondly, it will be easier to sell. Producers want something new and revolutionary – but not *that* new, and not *that* revolutionary. All the same, there is no point in (or market for) another musical saying what has been said before. What is needed is a new situation, or a new approach to an old situation – moon and June will never be successfully resurrected. You have to have an angle that is fresh, but do beware of taking a fad as your subject matter. If you start work now on 'Road Rage: The Musical', by the time it's finished it will be a historical curio, and not the long-awaited follow-up to *Starlight Express*.

**I name this show** …

A good title is important; it should inform and intrigue. Having distilled the concept of your show into a sentence or two, you need a title that reduces it to two or three words (with perhaps a strapline underneath of three or four more). *Passion*, for instance, does just that. *Camelot* is much more evocative than *The Once And Future King*, and *City of Angels* has a flavour of the period and genre.

Unfortunately, adapted works seem at present to be stuck in a groove of 'Source Work: The Musical'. If that is an indication of the wit and invention that has gone into the rest of the writing, it doesn't fill me with the compulsion to find out more!

# 2   Construction

When asked what were the three most important things to bear in mind when writing a musical, Oscar Hammerstein replied, 'Structure, structure and structure'.

## The Blueprint

The structure is how you organize the material and tell the story: the blueprint that incorporates the action, characters and dramatic premise. In architectural terms, you can't just order some bricks and start laying them, hoping that a viable building will arise by magic. Be warned by all those buildings which look as though that's what happened (in spite of the planning). Like erecting a building, writing a musical requires the successful planning of a conjunction of several individual skills and disciplines. What the blueprint does is to enable you to develop fully the potential of your original idea, to define what the scenes and songs are like, and what they must do. If it's not clear in your mind what you are trying to create before you start, you're unlikely to reach a successful conclusion. It's much more difficult to rework something after a false start than to write it properly in the first place.

Very few people have ever been multi-talented enough to write book, music and lyrics. The most recent was probably Lionel Bart, and the musical has become more complex in the last twenty-five years. When even Stephen Sondheim and Andrew Lloyd Webber (both ends of the spectrum, so to speak) collaborate with others, the message should be heeded. There are examples of people who have written all the words (book and lyrics), such as Alan Jay Lerner, or all the songs (music and lyrics), such as Jerry Herman, but usually there is a separate composer. The advantage of working alone may be that there are no arguments; but the disadvantage is that there is no help. So there are usually two or three collaborators; this in itself can be a problem, resulting in the arguments – which is another reason why you need a clear blueprint to work to.

## The Storyline

So, you have already had the inspiration and are armed with your concept – an idea, and a vision of how to develop it. Now for the perspiration. The structural planning process breaks down into two parts, the first of which is the storyline. This is a complete description of what happens, together with the biographical background of your characters. With this, you are defining precisely who the characters are and what happens to them.

A plot must not be a succession of unrelated incidents; it should be a pattern of interacting events – cause and effect. Nothing should happen by chance or coincidence; there must always be a reason or motivation. As E.M. Forster said, 'The King dies, then the Queen dies. That is a story. The King dies; then the Queen dies of grief. That is a plot.' However, you don't have to reveal everything at once. You can create mystery to keep your audience intrigued. You can hook them with a combination of suspense and surprise. (Suspense is when they know that there is a bomb under the table that may go off; surprise is when they don't, and it does.)

The plot has to have a satisfying dramatic shape in terms of character and story, following the three-part form of exposition, development and resolution (this is classically expressed as 'Boy meets girl; boy loses girl; boy finds girl).

*Exposition* introduces characters with whom the audience
will sympathize and in whom they will be interested.
It locates them in a situation which intrigues the
audience as to how it will turn out.

*Development* adds new and unforeseen twists to this
situation which will further puzzle the audience as to
what will happen. It should put the major characters
in jeopardy in a way that is not easily resolved, but the
audience must want them to triumph.

*Resolution* brings the story to a conclusion which is
realistic, satisfying and (hopefully) unexpected.

In terms of the overall length, this should roughly be in
the proportions of:

Exposition 25%: Development 50%: Resolution 25%.

You need to work on the storyline until you have given the
idea this shape. Both the characters and the story must be
developed in a sympathetic manner. When complete, the
storyline should tell you where and when the story is set,
how the show opens and closes, how the characters
develop, and what the action is. If you are adapting existing
material, it's a selection process – and this is the point to
make the selection. You may add extra characters or plots to
a simple idea, or refine down a vast story to manageable
proportions – there was a musical version of *Gone With the
Wind*.

Whether your story is original or an adaptation, it must
be specific. The characters and events must not just be
types, generalities and occurrences. You must ask yourself:

Why these events happen to these people. Every character must contribute to the advancement of the plot.

Why they occur in this place. There must be a specific
reason for the characters to be there (work, rest or
play).

Why they happen at this time. The action of your story
must start with the initiation of the event.

What is changed by them. Your story must be an *event*
which *happens*, not a situation which just exists.

Why can they happen in no other way. You must

convince your audience that yours is the only realistic outcome.

The story must arise from the intentions of the characters and be driven by their motivations. To be satisfying for an audience these motivations must be both exterior and interior. Consider *The Phantom of the Opera*. The exterior motivation is: what is it about? – the Phantom wants to make Christine a star (the plot). The interior motivation is: why does he do this? – he wants to be loved (spiritual growth). As the story progresses its momentum must increase. The conflict must build, so the obstacles that the hero must confront become greater, and the pace must accelerate, so they occur at more frequent intervals. Too many first attempts at writing fail because there is insufficient development. The story is too linear, with a lack of jeopardy, and is therefore one-dimensional.

Whatever the basic subject matter of your show, it usually involves a love story. Music appeals to the emotions and best fits an emotional story. As Mark Steyn says, 'When emotion outgrows the spoken word it becomes song; when it outgrows song, it becomes dance'. However, the most memorable love relationships on stage are not those of mutual adoration (which is dull) but those of sexual antagonism, where attraction expresses itself through hostility. Thus the obstacles to its successful conclusion come from the characters themselves. If this is not the case, then there must be a threat from outside – as in *West Side Story*.

## Audience Expectation

The members of the audience will feel cheated if you don't fulfil their expectations both as the story unfolds, and in the final outcome. They are a willing partner in a performance (after all, they chose to be there), but they make certain demands. You have to play fair with them. If they have been led to expect a confrontation, it must take place, it is a *scène à faire* – a climactic scene that cannot be omitted. Otherwise they will feel let down and lose interest.

A novel may jump forward in the development of a relationship, simply covering it with a sentence of explanation. On the stage, you must actually show this happening, putting in scenes that give characters the opportunity to grow. Always be on the lookout for important scenes that you may have missed out; you must deliver what you promise.

You can't start off with one set of characters and then kill them off halfway through, or start off with one story and then go off in a new direction. *Les Miserables* is the exception that proves the rule, and Boublil and Schonberg didn't try it twice. This doesn't mean that the story must be trite and predictable (that has to be avoided at all costs), but it must be believable, consistent and conclusive. You don't have to have a happy ending, but you must have a satisfactory one; in the musical version, Godot must arrive.

*Deus ex machina* (the intervention of divine providence, or an authoritarian figure, to untangle a plot that the author is unable to resolve in any other way) is not acceptable. The only exception is if the outside agency can be incorporated into the original premise (in which case it ceases to be genuine *deus ex machina*). Audiences will feel cheated by an unrealistic outcome. Musicals demand better construction and more discipline than plays.

## Sympathetic Characters

Audiences must become emotionally involved in your story, and they do this by identifying with the characters and situations you present. You should encourage them by creating sympathy – making your hero the victim of undeserved misfortune: physical (Cyrano de Bergerac), injustice (Jean Valjean), or loss, whether financial or personal (Sweeney Todd). He should also be likeable, charismatic and have desirable qualities: a good person, who is funny and good at what he does. Then, when you put him in jeopardy by either of the Aristotelian methods – *anagnorisis* (the disclosure of previously unknown facts), or *peripeteia* (a sudden reversal of fortune) – the audience will worry about the physical or emotional threat you have posed.

The character's positive side must be established at his introduction; the flaws which make him human should only be revealed later. Moreover, the point at which an audience receives information can be used to affect how they react. If they know only what the hero knows, they can share his struggle to find out what is going on, and this enables you to intrigue them by building in an element of surprise. If they know more than the hero knows, they can worry for him, and you can create a sense of anticipation.

## Signposting

Signposting or foreshadowing (planting early on a fact that will be needed later in the plot) enables you to get full value out of a crisis when it comes, and establishes motivation. You should make your characters' actions, in overcoming the obstacles you put in their path, believable and credible. This can be done by establishing their credentials during the exposition, in an unrelated and seemingly innocuous way. You know the sort of thing: 'Just back from your cookery class then, Mrs Lovatt?'

'Oh yes, Mr Todd – you'd be surprised what you can put into pies.'

Aim to get double value from everything which happens, so an event which is entertaining and interesting in itself also lays a mine that explodes later on. When something has immediate relevance an audience will not look too hard for its ultimate purpose, but it must be well disguised. Similarly, if events from early in the story are echoed in some way later on, you can use the opportunity for a reprise, and establish your character's growth.

## Plotting

The musical form can't be too complex. It needs one main plot, which is usually the love story, and probably two sub-plots to make it interesting – one of which must have humour. Sub-plots must function as a stand-alone story, but should also contribute to the main plot, and thus should be an integral part of the main storyline. Very often in the classic shows there are three couples, each with a plot-line. The leads are the romantic couple, who are not usually allowed to be funny. The second leads have the main comedy scenes and numbers. The third leads are older, either a married couple or 'second-time-arounders', giving you a different viewpoint that combines comedy and romance. This is true of *She Loves Me* and *Me and My Girl*. Sometimes there is a fourth couple with a stronger dramatic storyline, as in *Showboat*.

You need to be very fluid at the storyline stage, and try any number of ways of developing the material. You may not get it right at first. Almost all the great writing teams of the time tried to turn *Pygmalion* into a musical and failed after Lerner and Lowe gave up their first attempt. As you work, you must guard against situations that are unbelievable, actions that are out of character and scenes that either do not advance the story or are too long for their entertainment value. What you leave out is as important as what you put in.

People often get impatient and, having arrived at a concept, want to launch into writing scenes or songs without thinking it through any further. That's jumping from the foundations to the roof, without building the walls. What can happen is that you write the wrong songs. You may write a good song, but, because you haven't defined what its dramatic purpose is, it doesn't fit in the final book. In that case, you either have to lose it (and you've wasted the effort), or you keep it, and it doesn't work properly. Probably the most common fault with new writers is that they write the wrong songs.

## Song Points

Collaborators now look at the best way to tell the story, employing either dialogue or song, as they develop the storyline. This has superseded the old fashioned way of writing a book and then 'spotting' song points.

Song ideas are crucial. Singing something gives it weight and importance. You must be sure that the idea is strong enough to carry that weight. You should give very careful consideration as to precisely what to musicalize, trying to avoid the obvious and what has been done before. Don't make life hard for yourself by attempting a song on a subject or situation about which there is nothing new (or nothing at all) left to say. Certain events will suggest themselves as musical moments. Songs can extract extra value from dramatic climaxes, and should define the emotional peaks of the story.

Having established where those moments are, second, third or even fourth thoughts may be necessary before you hit on exactly the right song idea. Most writers can give examples of different numbers for a particular slot. The record is believed to be held by Kander and Ebb in *Flora – The Red Menace* with twenty. Apparently Sondheim always referred to 'Maria' in *West Side Story* as 'the cigarette number', because he and Bernstein wanted to change it, but couldn't come up with another idea, so each night during the previews they used to go out to the lobby for a cigarette.

## Nuts and bolts

There are a number of basic ground rules you need to observe as you put your storyline together. There are certain key points in a show which it is vital to get right.

Musicals are generally presented in two acts. There are exceptions: *A Chorus Line*, *Follies*, *Man of La Mancha*, *Passion*, *1776* and *Grand Hotel* have no interval. This is not generally popular with theatre-owners, who lose bar sales, and in the first four cases they insisted that an interval be inserted (this is commercial theatre!). *The Apple Tree, The Boy Friend* and *The Amazons* have two intervals. The average length of musicals, though, means that two acts is the most appropriate form, and the second act should be shorter than the first. Overall running time should ideally be no more than two-and-a-half hours; anything over three hours is heavily frowned upon, as the band would be on overtime. Ninety pages is about the right length for a script – fifty for the first act and forty for the second. (I knew that the original version of *Jeeves* wouldn't work as soon as I saw the script, because it was about an inch thick.)

Conventionally, musicals begin and end each act with music. You must have a very good dramatic reason to depart from this. Openings are the most important and the most difficult part of the show to write – and usually the most rewritten part of the show. Many people say that the opening should be written last (you don't start designing a house with the front door).

You not only have to establish the time and place of the action, introduce the theme of the plot and the principal characters, but also establish the conventions in which you are going to present your work. Openings tend to show either a character who is at the peak of his powers doing what he does well (so we can soon see him face a crisis), or else a character entering a strange new world (so we can find out what will happen to him). Either way, some sort of sung and spoken montage using the full company allows you to cover a lot of ground very quickly.

Few numbers have managed to combine all this so skilfully as 'Tradition' in *Fiddler on The Roof* – where the very title encompasses the theme. The process is also cleverly handled in *La Cage aux Folles*, where 'We Are What We Are' introduces the Cagelles, and 'A Little More Mascara' transforms Albin into Zaza. But what is an audience expected to understand from a number called 'How Do You Spell Ambassador?' launching *High Society*? The only dancing opening is in *A Chorus Line*, but that rehearsal piano and single word – bo bom, bo bom, bom bom; 'Again' – says it all. *Oklahoma!* is the exception to all the rules: it opens with an empty stage and Curly singing 'Oh What a Beautiful Mornin'' from the wings. If you choose to use the technique of flashback, as in *Aspects of Love*, you increase your problems, because your opening has to establish the *now* as well as the *then*.

The second most difficult thing to get right is the Act I

finale. The act must end with a crisis of such cataclysmic proportions, that your audience will be impatient to return from the bar to find out how it is to be resolved. (The interval is their only real opportunity to escape, so you must see to it that they don't want to take their chance!) So, far from being a rounding off, a good first-act finale should actually give a sense of something starting. Consider how 'A Little Priest' hatches the plot of people in pies and sets up what is to come in *Sweeney Todd*. In *Annie*, 'You Won't be an Orphan for Long', tells us that Act II will be about the search for her parents. One of the best Act I closers ever, 'One Day More' in *Les Miserables* draws together the various strands of the story and builds a sense of coming conflagration. Contrast this with *Sunday in the Park with George*, where 'Sunday' builds to a dazzling and thrilling climax, but is definitely the end of the show – there is nowhere else it can go.

Act II openings must gather the audience's attention, move the show up a gear and mark a decisive step in the story development. There is frequently a time lapse or change of circumstance from the end of Act I. The action of Act II in *Aspects of Love* is twelve years later. In *Into the Woods* (with 'So Happy') we find that, love having triumphed, this is where the cracks begin to appear. A similar technique is used with 'This Plum is Too Ripe' in *The Fantasticks*.

The next important moment is the Point of Resolution, where the story starts to conclude. Frequently, in the classic shows, this is where the ballet is. In *The King and I*, 'The Small House of Uncle Thomas' is interrupted with the news of Lun Tha's capture. In *West Side Story*, 'Somewhere' recapitulates the story before it moves to its climax. The idea of a ballet was not completely abandoned. It continued in a more modest form with 'Tick Tock' in *Company* and 'The Music and the Mirror' in *A Chorus Line*. The point of resolution is also the place for what is known as 'the eleven o'clock number' (a hangover from the days when shows started and finished later and it was 11 p.m. by the time this point was reached.) Often – because this is the strongest emotional turning point, and therefore a particularly appropriate moment for a song – this is the show's best-known number: for example 'I'm a Brass Band' in *Sweet Charity*, 'Time Heals Everything' in *Mack and Mabel*, and 'I'll Never Fall in Love Again' in *Promises, Promises*. In many shows the title number fills this slot – 'Cabaret', 'Hello Dolly' and 'Kiss of the Spider Woman', for instance.

The Act II finale must round off the piece satisfactorily and show how far the characters and story have travelled. It must be emotionally satisfying. If not happy, then it should be uplifting, enlightening or hopeful. This is usually achieved by a reprise of some sort, since it is too late to introduce new material. It can be the opening number, as in *Cabaret* and *Aspects of Love*; the title song, as in *Camelot* and *Windy City*; the principal character's big number, as in *Man of La Mancha* and *City of Angels*; or, in the case of *Joseph*, the whole show. It is good if you can save some sort of surprise (such as the trick ending in *A Chorus Line*) to show you haven't run out of ideas. You should aim to both confirm and confound your audience's expectations. Ideally a musical should be based on the Disneyland principal: just when you think you've seen everything, something else happens to top it.

## Book shows versus through-written

Before starting, you should think very carefully about the form you work in. Because Andrew Lloyd Webber and Boublil and Schonberg have been so successful in reaching what is really a non-theatregoing audience with their through-written style, everyone is jumping on the bandwagon. But this does not necessarily mark a turning-point in the evolution of musicals. It may be just a fashion, like rock musicals a few years ago. Mark Steyn, mourning that new musicals have become 'dialogue-free zones', debates the advisability of musicalizing 'Shall I make some coffee?'. As he says, would the impact of 'Some Enchanted Evening' have been the same if the words had been 'Would you like a biscuit?'

Musicals should not aspire to become opera; they are better than opera. The musical is a total theatrical experience, with dialogue, music or dance as appropriate to the moment. Opera is music, with the rest tacked on; ballet is dance, with the rest tacked on. Only the musical is a totally integrated form. A song should fulfil a specific function in character or plot development, so you don't have all the characters eventually singing the same tune, but with different words. Again, Mark Steyn says, 'A through-sung score is not subjected to the same scrutiny as individual songs in a book show and lapses almost inevitably into generality. You rarely feel that the music is a deeply personal, unconscious revelation of character.'

Look at two shows which played concurrently – *Grand Hotel* and *Aspects of Love* – and contrast their effectiveness. In *Grand Hotel* the music content was increased to the point where the orchestra hardly stopped playing, yet each song or musical fragment was justified by its contribution to the storytelling. In *Aspects Of Love*, it felt as though the score had simply been sliced up like salami and spread out on a platter, with songs repeated regularly just to drum them into the audience's head, so that they could go out whistling them. The artistic versus the commercial. Think, too, of *South Pacific*, where the themes keep recurring, but for specific reasons. The reprise is a valid technique if it makes a comment on what is happening – if the character or the story is reliving or reassessing a past moment. The point of a reprise is to add something new, not just to repeat something; either the same character has a different view, or a different character now has the same view. This can work in a variety of ways. Repeating the same lyric can emphasize how far a character has travelled by taking on a completely different meaning, and the effectiveness of this can be increased by changing the time signature or arrangement of the music. The best example is 'Let Me Entertain You' in *Gypsy*: it is first heard sung by the child Baby June, then by the adult Dainty June, and finally as a strip number by Louise as Gypsy herself. Alternatively, a different lyric can offer a character the opportunity to reflect on what has happened since the same tune was heard before, and how much he has changed. One character singing another character's song can signal a change of attitude.

Nothing written here will stop people using the through-written form willy-nilly, any more than it will prevent them from ransacking French literature for another *Les Miserables*. Success doesn't lie in repeating a formula (unless you are repeating your own, as in *Miss Saigon* and *Martin Guerre*). It will be a shame if people are so dazzled by Andrew Lloyd Webber's monetary success that they use the through-written form regardless, rather than dispassionately assessing whether that is the most effective way of telling a particular story.

Another thing to consider is that by the end of your two-year development time through-written shows will have been done to death, and people will want book shows again. There's nothing truer than 'everything old is new again'. Hal Prince, talking about *Kiss of the Spider Woman*, said that he thought the book musical was making a comeback, and the success of *Crazy for You* and *City of Angels*, after a string of through-written flops, may well have turned attention back to book shows.

## Character Background

As you develop the storyline you should write yourself a detailed Character Background for each character – their story so far. This helps you to put flesh on the bones, and will enable you to know how characters will react in each situation. It will also help you to determine how they will express themselves, in both dialogue and lyric. You can include typical attitudes and phrases, so that, when you come to write, you will already know how your characters think and talk. Figure 2 gives an example.

Remember that characters must have names appropriate to the period and status of their origins. This means no one called Wendy born before 1904 (the first production of *Peter Pan*), and no one called Kylie (ever!). Leave descriptive names like Sir Politick Would-be and Lady Wishfort to the seventeenth century.

46

## Figure 2 Character Background

---

### *That Sinking Feeling*

---

**SAM O. BALUSTRADE**

*The* Hollywood producer specializing in cheap thrillers – e.g. *The Knife*.
*What does the 'O' stand for? – nothing*.
Murdered wife and distributed her body in his luggage, intending to dispose
  of her overboard.
Dresses up as Amarylla (deceased wife) to fool people that she is still alive.
Dismisses Nazi threat – *What are they going to do, kill us all?*
Motto: Never say die.
Secret in Hatbox: Severed head.


**RUBY RODRIGUEZ**

Failed actress and torch singer whose flame is about to be extinguished –
  suffering from a terminal and incurable disease.
Has been working in the cabarets of Berlin; also opera, which she hated – *It
  was Weill*.
Never liked the guy with the small moustache and the rather stiff wave.
Returning to New York to die in a manner to which she would like to have
  been accustomed.
Motto: There is a financial solution to every problem.
Secret in hatbox: Pet crocodile named Ziegfeld – *I was growing him into a
  matching set of luggage, but I may have to settle for a handbag and
  shoes*.


**BERKLEY FARQHUAR**

Earl of Rottingdean, known as Pongo.
Reluctant honeymooner – married Bunty as must produce an heir.
Educated at Lagby with the Captain and Kurt – unhealthy interest in
  fagging.
Thanks to the abdication (both legs), has rocketed up to fourth in line to the
  throne.
Intimate of Nancy Mitford – joined the Black Shorts.
Accidentally swapped with the Captain as a baby and really the son of the
  Butler and the Cook – so his bride is also his sister.
Motto: *Noblesse oblige*.
Secret in hatbox: Family jewels (known as the Brighton Rocks).

### SISTER HENRIETTA TEMPLE DAY
American evangelist (retired).

About to give up being a Sister to become a mother (result of indiscretion with the Captain at the 'Where Were You When The Ship Went Down' party on the inward journey.

Returning from European fund-raising trip, which went disastrously wrong at the casino in Monte Carlo when she bet everything on red and it came up black.

*You can't interest the Italians in religion – they're all Catholics.*

Motto: Never trust a sailor.

Secret in hatbox: Gin bottle.


### CAPTAIN STEWART COOK
Rightful heir to Rottingdean estate.

Newly promoted after his predecessor hit something in the Channel (the Isle of Wight).

Ran away to sea as a result of an unpleasant incident in the dorm at Lagby school.

Straight as a plank – and twice as thick.

Motto: Press on regardless.

Secret in hatbox: Rubber ring (he is afraid of water).


### HELGA VON DOPPLEDECKER
A very simple German maiden, unknowingly enmeshed in a vile Nazi plot.

Escaping from Germany with the secret formula of Hitler's breakfast cereal – *Haven't you heard of wheatgerm warfare?*

Stowing away in the hope of finding Kurt – *Mine childhood sweetbread.*

Motto: Remember Mönchengladbach.

Secret in hatbox: Secret formula.

---

In order to avoid libel suits from real people who share the character's name (but not proclivities), writers often resort to a gazetteer as inspiration. For instance, Augustus Sheringham, Lady Camberley and Lord Brighton (the well known peer).

## Well-laid plans

It is important that you spend time exploring your ideas before you actually start to write. Alan Ayckbourn says that he spends nine months planning something before committing himself to dialogue. It then takes him a week to complete – it may take you a little longer. You will undoubtedly change the piece as you develop it, but it's much more difficult to change your way of looking at something once you've actually committed yourself by writing the scene or the song, than it is to get the structure correct and write what you need first time round.

When you are satisfied with the storyline and characters, you can move on to the second stage in the structural planning process, the Scene Breakdown, which is dealt with in the next chapter. (You have just learnt another lesson: the cliff-hanger makes people want to find out what happens next!)

# 3   The Book

Definition: the book writer is the person whose fault it is. If the story doesn't make sense – rewrite the book. If the characters aren't sympathetic – rewrite the book. If the numbers aren't working – rewrite the book, because the lead-in must be wrong. If the reviews are good, it's because of the great actors; if the reviews are bad, it's because the book was poor.

The book is the spine that supports the body of the show, whether it has dialogue or is through-written. It is the framework on which the words (spoken or sung) hang. Shows now tend to have a higher music-to-dialogue ratio than the classic Rodgers and Hammerstein shows, which usually have a number every four pages, but nothing is written in blood (not until the dress rehearsal stage, when there will probably be plenty of it around). As you develop your story, you must decide on the most effective way to tell it, be it large-scale or small or through-written. Suit the action to the word, the word to the action.

## The Scene Breakdown

Having successfully completed the storyline, you can now move on to the Scene Breakdown. Those expecting to start writing at this point will be disappointed. In the building, we're up to the plumbing and wiring – this is how you avoid the light coming on when you turn on the shower.

The scene breakdown divides the storyline into specific

scenes. It lets you develop the characters and plotlines. For each scene you should list the time, location, characters and what happens. Figure 3 shows an example. You should start the scene as late in the story as possible. Don't waste two pages indicating that something is about to happen – just get on with it. Each scene should contain:

one or more plot points,
and/or a song,
and/or comedy/dramatic action.

Plot points are new information which help to move the story forward; they can be conveyed in dialogue or song. Remember that it is always better for the audience to see something happen, than to hear about it. For this reason, using a narrator for your story is usually a bad idea.

In the same way that the story as a whole must have a shape, so must each scene. When it reaches a conclusion it must stop, and not be allowed to dribble away. You should start with a positive action or statement, build up to a climax, and end with one of:

a joke,
a surprise (good news) or shock (bad news),
a pointer to the next scene or action (e.g. 'I'm going to find out'),
a song.

It is particularly good to end with a song, because it can contain any or all of the others, and the subsequent scene change produces a natural break for the audience to respond. You need to construct these opportunities for them to release their emotions, so that they can continue to give their attention. Without such opportunities they feel left out – and you need them to feel involved.

Whether your story is mostly serious, or mostly comic, it must have elements of both to succeed. You cannot sustain one dramatic level throughout the whole action.

# Figure 3 Scene Breakdown

## ACT I *Around the World in Eighty Days*

| Scene | Location | Characters | Plot | Number |
|---|---|---|---|---|
| 1 | Reform Club | Perkins, Flanagan, Lord A, Stuart, Ralph, Sullivan, Fogg, Passepartout. | Set up Club – Ralph arrives – Fogg appears – News of robbery – Passepartout appears and is hired – play cards – discuss robbery – Fogg makes bet. | 'At The Club' 'Eighty Days' |
| 2A | Street | Passepartout, Foster. | Passepartout's philosophy – arrives Savile Row – meets Foster. | 'Time Does Not Permit' |
| 2B | Savile Row | Passepartout, Fogg. | Announce bet – pack. | |
| 2C | Charing Cross | Flanagan, Ralph, Stuart, Fogg, Passepartout, Guard. | Departure. | |
| 2D | European journey | Fogg, Passepartout, Guards, Passengers. | Rush through each place – Fogg optimistic/Passepartout pessimistic. | 'Time Does Not Permit' |

| | | | | |
|---|---|---|---|---|
| 3 | Suez Consul | Consul, Fix, Fogg, Servant. | Introduce Fix – Fix mistakes Fogg for robber. | |
| 4 | Deck of *Mongolia* | Fix, Purser, Passepartout. | Fix philosophy – Fix meets Passepartout. | 'Trav'lin' ' |
| 5 | Fogg's cabin | Fogg, Passepartout. | Fogg philosophy. | 'Travel Alone' |
| 6A | Bombay, Consul | Consul, Fix, Fogg, Servant. | Fix fails to stop Fogg. | |
| 6B | Bombay, street | Fix, Passepartout. | Fix waylays Passepartout. | |
| 6C | Bombay, Consul | Consul, Aouda. | Introduce Aouda. | |
| 6D | Bombay, street | Aouda, uncle, priests. | Aouda's situation – uncle abducts Aouda. | 'Person Wanted' |
| 7 | Train For Calcutta | Fogg, Cromarty, Passepartout. | Introduce Cromarty – Fogg background – Passepartout nearly misses train. | |
| 8 | Bundlekhand, jungle | Fogg, Cromarty, Passepartout, Parsee, Aouda, uncle, priests. | Train halted – Start walking – Hire elephant – Suttee – Passepartout and Fogg rescue Aouda. | Underscore Suttee |

Contrast is needed: short and long scenes, sung and spoken sequences, and varied types of scene. The effect should be like a rollercoaster – emotional or comic peaks should be followed by a rest. This is the porter-in-*Macbeth* syndrome: in *West Side Story*, 'Gee, Officer Krupke' fulfils this role; 'Herod's Song', the only non-dramatic number in *Jesus Christ Superstar*, provides an element of humour before the trial; and in *Les Miserables* Thenardier, the innkeeper, and his wife are all that stand between the audience and three-and-a-quarter hours of unrelenting gloom.

Humour is an important element in any show, but it must be taken seriously. It should be truthful and real, and it should come naturally from the character or situation, not be imposed on it. It's not true that 'it doesn't matter, it's only a gag'. Cheap laughs and obvious jokes are not required, and 'funny' names, scenery, costumes and props are especially to be avoided – they are a sign of desperation.

When you write you should have some idea of staging in mind, to help you focus your ideas – even though the show will probably not end up being done that way. There will always be many ways of staging any piece of work (we've had four hundred years of Shakespeare productions, with none of them the same), but you should remember that words are not the only thing – you must think in pictures and actions, too. Most dramatic situations can only be fully appreciated when they are acted out – when we can see the reactions of the other characters, and when we hear the vocal colour of the actor delivering the line.

As well as dramatic needs, you must consider practical things – like not having a character ending one scene in one location and one costume and then starting the next somewhere else and dressed differently. Don't bind your imagination too much, but also avoid making hopelessly impractical design demands. Ignore Sam Goldwyn's entreaty to 'start with an earthquake and build up to a climax'.

Stage directions should be included only when

absolutely necessary. You should make your intentions clear if there is room for ambiguity, but don't underline *every* stress, or qualify (pedantically, repeatedly, and at ponderous length that goes well beyond that which is necessary) how every sentence is to be delivered. Leave something for the actors to do. Restrict your directions to making clear when lines are concurrent, private or specifically directed.

Since everything is going to be new to your audience, you must make sure that they have grasped both the plot points and your characters' names and relationships straight away. If they don't quickly understand what is going on they will lose interest in what follows. You do this by repetition and emphasis. Don't forget the rule of three: tell them what you're going to say, say it, then tell them what you said. For example:

A:    I know who killed Miss Scarlet.
B:    Who?
A:    It was Colonel Mustard.
B:    Colonel Mustard killed Miss Scarlet!
A:    Yes. Colonel Mustard killed Miss Scarlet in the library, with a lump of lead piping.
B:    In the library with a lump of lead piping? But how?
A:    Simple really when you think about it …

It was good enough for Shakespeare, so it should be good enough for you; don't overdo it, though.

Clues as to where and when the action is taking place (and how it relates to what has gone before) should be incorporated into the opening of each scene. Members of the audience shouldn't have to scrabble around in their programmes to find this out. But you must take care to give the information with some subtlely; as with all exposition, the audience must absorb the knowledge without realizing that it is doing so. But do beware of characters who spend more time explaining the story to each other than participating in it. Remember that Hortense's telephone conversation at the opening of *The Boy Friend* is, like the whole show, a spoof of an outdated genre. Try to avoid resurrecting it.

You need to devote a great deal of attention to getting your characters on and off the stage convincingly. You must have a satisfactory explanation for both the actors and the audience. People cannot just appear for no reason (like the jolly villagers). Actors will want to know:

What do I know at this entrance?
Why have I come on?
Why am I going off?

The nature of entrances and exits can define character. The bumbling character shambles on at the wrong moment in the middle of someone else's scene; the powerful character strides on and takes command of the stage. Similarly, an exit can be made with an apology or a curse.

## The songs

When you have completed the scene breakdown you should finalize the song points. That is, you should list where each song goes, what it does, who sings it, and what type of song it is, by means of a Song Analysis (like that in Figure 4).

There should be variety both in terms of the number of singers – solo/duet/trio/chorus – and types of numbers – ballad/rhythm/comedy(point). The songs must be placed correctly, usually starting and ending each act with a bright number, and with succeeding numbers in different styles, sung by different characters. You don't want three ballads coming along one after another like number 31 buses, or a character who sings three times in Act I and never opens his mouth in Act II. Similarly, a variety of types of song should be given to each character; you can give depth to a character by using different types of songs to show different facets of the personality.

Songs must grow from the situation or character, and not be imposed upon it. As with dialogue, they are either active or reflective. Active songs forward the plot: 'What shall I do? I'll do this!' Reflective songs tell you something

## Figure 4  Song Analysis

---

### Sharp Focus

| Scene | Song | Characters | Type | Content |
|---|---|---|---|---|
| **Act I**: | | | | |
| 1 Prologue | 'Expo' | All. | Fast rhythm montage | Entire story |
| 2 Studio | 'Sharp Focus' | Charlie, Peter, Nick, Biggs. | Rhythm | Philosophies |
| 3 Beach | 'Sunset Therapy' | Charlie, Peter. | Jazz ballad | Seduction |
| 4 Studio | 'My Diary' | Diana. | Laundry list | Comic |
| 5 Apartment | 'Missing' | Charlie, Peter. | Jazz waltz | Setting up house |
| 6 Dark Room | 'Something More' | Charlie. | Ballad | Questioning |
| 7 Ski Slope/ Studio | The Argument | Peter, Charlie, Nick, Diana. | Rhythm | Explosive |
| 8 Studio | 'Pictures' | Charlie. | Ballad | Despair |
| **Act II**: | | | | |
| 1 Restaurant Studio | 'Profile' | All. | Fast rhythm montage | Time lapse |
| 2 Studio | 'Moments' | Peter. | Rhythm | Explanation |
| 3 Airport | 'After All' | Charlie. | Ballad | Resignation |
| 4 Restaurant | 'Leaving Her' | Charlie, Nick, Diana, Peter | Rhythm | Argument |
| 5 Hotel | 'Together' | Charlie, Peter. | Jazz ballad | Reconciliation |
| 6 Gallery | 'Expo' | All. | Fast rhythm montage | Entire story Recap |

---

new about the characters – sometimes in an oblique fashion, since the character may not understand the situation, or may not be telling the truth. Either way, by the end of the song the situation must have changed. There is no other reason for a song. It does not repeat what you have just seen or heard in the scene, nor provide light relief from the plot; if it has nothing new to say, you don't need it. This advice was not heeded by Howard Goodall in his Spanish civil war piece *Days of Hope*. At the end of each scene there was a song repeating what had just happened, sung by all the characters, whether they were in the scene or not.

The joins from dialogue to song and back again should be seamless. You should not be able to tell where the book-writer stops and the lyricist starts. Joseph Stein says he has written dialogue which has become a lyric, citing 'Do You Love Me?' from *Fiddler on the Roof*. The lyric of 'Surrey with a Fringe on Top' comes straight out of the dialogue in *Green Grow The Lilacs*, the original source material of *Oklahoma!* Stephen Sondheim always asks his book writer to write the scene for the song point, which he then rewrites using song and dialogue.

Perhaps it would be useful to define the difference between a play with music, and a musical play. In a play with music, if you took out the musical element you would still have a play. Think, for example, of *The Blue Angel*: the songs enhanced the atmosphere of 1920s Berlin, and they added texture, but they were not germane to the plot. Similarly, the songs in *Piaf* gave you the opportunity to experience the character on stage, but the play was about her off-stage life. With a musical, or musical play, if you took away the musical element, what remained would be meaningless.

People don't always appreciate the difference between pop songs and show songs. Once upon a time they were the same thing, but since the 1950s they have each moved in different directions. My definition is that the most important thing about a pop song is the sound, while the most important thing about a show song is the meaning. Lyrics are often the last thing to be added to a pop song, after the music track is finished, and their importance is certainly less than it once was. With show songs the lyrics have become both more complex, and more specific to the moment. The result is that there are now hardly any 'liftable' songs that can exist outside the context of the show. You are unlikely to have a number one hit, unless it has a remarkably bland theme, like 'Love Changes Everything'. The other main difference is that show songs must be resolved by the end. In pop songs the situation usually remains unchanged, the singer is usually still wanting someone or looking for someone.

## Character

Character is the essence of musical theatre, because music can pin-point mood, emotion and motivation more precisely than words. Character is defined by:

> *Physical make up*: sex, appearance and abilities,
> *Personality*: intelligence and emotional make up,
> *Background*: interests, enthusiasms and the sum of their personal experiences to date, usually expressed as nature and nurture.

Character is revealed by temperament, behaviour and attitude.

The main characters should initiate events. Beware of minor characters grabbing the best lines and numbers, and keep all major characters keyed into the action as much as possible. Follow through the story of each of the characters separately, scene by scene; they must have a positive contribution to make to a scene, or they shouldn't be in it. To help you to do this, you should draw up a Character Plot as shown in Figure 5.

The characters must be original, consistent, believable and interesting – you must defy cliché. You should ensure that all characters are well contrasted, to avoid confusion, and you should use as few as possible to tell your story, for reasons of economy – both dramatic and financial.

## Figure 5   Character Plot

---

### *Around the World in Eighty Days*

### Phileas Fogg

**Act I**

| *Scene* | *Character development* |
| --- | --- |

---

| 1 Club | Typically English, very straight, black and white; obsessed with time, impressed with Passepartout because of watch; whist enthusiast, enjoys calculating the odds of wager. |
| --- | --- |
| 2A Street | |
| 2B Savile Row | Changing routine – first sign of character change. |
| 2C Station | Sets off with composure, confident and assured. |
| 2D Journey | Single-minded no thought of failure. |
| 3 Suez, Consul | Condescending to Consul and Fix. |
| 4 Deck of *Mongolia* | |
| 5 Cabin | Icy, aloof, does not mix with others (no relationship with Passepartout), afraid of personal involvement; expounds philosophy – travel alone. |
| 6A Bombay, Consul | Steamrollers Consul and Fix. |
| 6B Bombay, street | |
| 6C Bombay, Consul | |
| 6D Bombay, street | |
| 7 Train for Calcutta | Background – poor relationship with father; prepared to leave without Passepartout. |

| | |
|---|---|
| 8 Bundlekhand, jungle | Resourceful, prepared to walk; pragmatic – hires elephant; change of character – heroic attempt to rescue Aouda. |
| 9 Train For Calcutta | Embarrassment at physical contact; retreats into shell, hides behind duty. |
| 10 Calcutta | Swashbuckling – in accepting responsibility for Aouda (not actually necessary) and dealing with Judge; warmer relationship with Passepartout. |
| 11 Deck of *Rangoon* | First sign of Aouda/Fogg/Passepartout triangle. |
| 12 Cabin | Beginning of relationship with Aouda; annoyance yet respect over being beaten at cards; unable to communicate. |
| 13 Hong Kong | Irritation and embarrassment at losing Aouda and Passepartout and missing ship. |

Characters should be slightly larger than life. *West Side Story* cranked up the emotional temperature of Romeo and Juliet. Tybalt (killed by Romeo) was Juliet's cousin, whereas Bernardo (killed by Tony) is not only Maria's brother, but also Anita's lover. This gives the character that extra motivational twist.

Some people say that ensemble shows (like *A Chorus Line* and *Grand Hotel*) inevitably engage the audience's sympathy less. Multiple characters mean that each plot-line has to be more simplistic, since there is less time for it to develop. This is something you should consider as you develop your story.

True depth of character demands that, as in life, most people are not all black or all white, but a realistic mixture of the two. If you are adapting an existing story, you may need to flesh out a one-dimensional character with new passions and skills to make him live on the musical stage. Go for the quirky, but be wary of someone who belongs to both the British National Party and Greenpeace. Characters must develop, but not change fundamentally. Growth arises from what they learn as a result of experiencing the events in the plot, which changes how they view and act in the situations which follow. The story should therefore involve a spiritual journey, but by the end the characters must still be the same people. Make sure, though, that you don't give away in Act I how they will develop in Act II.

All is as true for the other characters as it is for the hero, although minor characters cannot be explored in such detail. Think of character development in terms of photographic development. The action must be like the developing bath: it works continuously until your characters are removed and transferred to the fixer of the finale. (You could say that they are then washed by the applause of the audience in the curtain calls, but good taste prevents.)

Characters are established not only by their actions, but by the way they express themselves. As Henry Higgins says in *Pygmalion*,

> Men begin in Kentish Town with eighty pounds a year and end in Park Lane with a hundred thousand. They want to drop Kentish Town, but they give themselves away every time they open their mouths.

In the *My Fair Lady* lyric he expresses this sentiment in half the number of words – and they rhyme!

When you speak to a stranger on the telephone you immediately build up a mental picture of what the other person is like (not always a correct one, of course), based on the information you receive. You must create just such a picture of your characters and convey this to the audience. This is done with vocabulary (including slang or jargon), syntax (idiom), accent and speech rhythm/pattern. When you are working on your character background, you must decide the language that they will use.

Language is a living thing, constantly changing and re-inventing itself. You must therefore be certain that you use the correct vocabulary for someone of the class and period of your story. Since they have no sense of either, just watch any American mini-series set in non-contemporary England; see how the inappropriate words zing out at you, ruining the credibility of the story. Slang, jargon and idiomatic expressions are useful in establishing the milieu of your characters, but must be used sparingly; unless they are comprehensible to the 'civilian' general public, the audience will quickly become bored by it. When *Me and My Girl* crossed the Atlantic, an explanation had to be added of what cockney rhyming slang was and how it worked. Fortunately the toffs in the show were as mystified by working-class language as the American audience, so this could be done quite realistically.

## Dialogue

Characters must not make speeches – they must speak, and speech must have spontaneity. If you listen carefully to a real-life conversation you will be amazed by how often people fail to finish sentences; either they dry up, or lose the thread of what they are saying. Sometimes the other person (understanding the full meaning before all the words have been spoken) jumps in with a response. Try secretly taping conversations and see what a jumble it becomes.

Writing dialogue is a compromise between reality – which on the stage would be incomprehensible (or too tedious to command the attention of an audience) – and the perfectly crafted artificiality of a novel. You should push the audience as far as you can, though. It is certainly possible to have some overlapping dialogue, and to have two conversations taking place simultaneously, provided it makes a specific point – but not for the whole evening.

In general, dialogue must be sharper, wittier and more succinct than real life. It must be as interesting and amusing as the character will permit (bearing in mind that not every character can be lifted from an Oscar Wilde play). You must eliminate hesitation, verbosity and meandering, unless you are making a specific point about a character (and even then you must use it sparingly). You should write dialogue as you want it spoken ("e were right taken by 'e') but not phonetically. Establishing when a character is introduced that he has a French accent means that you can avoid writing the whole script in franglais.

Dialogue must pass a speakability test. If *you* can't say it, don't expect an actor to. Dialogue only lives when it is spoken, in the same way that lyrics only live when they are sung. Don't let your characters get carried away with the sound of their own voices, though. Economy should be your watchword; every line must be either active (advancing the plot) or reflective (illuminating the character).

Clichés should obviously be avoided, but beware also of the latest buzz word – which will probably have become a cliché by the time your show reaches a stage. Write with an eye to the future, and avoid excessive trendiness that will soon become outdated (unless trendiness is the thing you are trying to convey). Nothing changes faster than fashion; don't let your work become the hot pants of musical theatre. Walk the line between richness of language and staleness of overuse.

Dialogue must be couched in an individual style for each character. If yours is easily interchangeable between characters, then you haven't done it properly. Don't write similar speeches that it is easy for actors to confuse (they will find enough land mines of their own without your help). The worst first night I was ever part of was a production of *Blithe Spirit*. Elvira (the ghost of the leading man's first wife) makes similar appearances in each of the three acts. Unfortunately the actress playing Elvira was not one hundred percent sure of her lines and completely scrambled the different scenes. Buried within them were important plot points, so she managed to confuse not only herself but the rest of the cast, who began improvising wildly. Eventually someone pitched a line which allowed them to get back into the right scene, but nobody knew what they had said, or how much had been missed out. The audience must have been mystified. I certainly was, and I knew 'whodunnit'.

Dialogue must be like a tennis match. What one person says determines how the other responds, which in turn affects the next response, and so on. Each time, the conversation edges forward, until the end of the scene is reached. Dialogue must contain not just its immediate meaning, but an underlying message (the subtext). For instance, a character may not be able to talk about what really concerns him, and so indulges in small talk – as in 'Barcelona' from *Company*. Alternatively, a character may make a definite statement, but in a way which indicates that he feels, believes or fears that the opposite is true. Such obliquity will add depth and texture to your work. Don't go too far, though; the world is not yet ready for a Pinter musical.


## Check the plots

When you have completed the Scene Breakdown, Character Plot and Song Analysis, you need to test them out from a number of different angles. Firstly, story and character development. Do they fulfil the rule of Exposition/Development/Resolution, and are they logically developed and fully rounded, with no loose ends or inconsistencies? Secondly, the songs. Are they correctly placed and sufficiently varied in the context both of the whole show and of the individual characters?

You should then use these cross-reference plots, together with the Storyline, to prove to yourself that the idea for your show will really work. Only when you are convinced that it is sound should you start writing as such. What you will have done is to draw up a set of instructions for yourself, to define what you should be writing: the blueprint. For each scene you will know: how it starts, who's in it, how they get on and off, what happens, how it ends, and what the overall mood and intention is. Similarly for the songs, you will have defined the purpose, type and sound before you put pen to paper or finger to keyboard.

## Writing at last!

When you do start writing the scenes, you should use a similarly methodical approach. Firstly sketch in dialogue to get you through the basic shape. Then go back and make it as interesting as you can. You do this by refining the expression (vocabulary/speech pattern) and revealing the motivation and attitude of each character; creating obstacles (to make it less direct) and adding humour (if appropriate). As the script progresses, and you learn more about the characters and their story, you will revise each scene making it denser. You can add layers of meaning, revealing more about character background and motivation, and ensuring that actions taking place later in the story are consistent with and firmly founded on the information contained in the early scenes.

You will find it much easier to write to a carefully defined brief like this than literally to make it up as you go along. What is more important, you will be able to write more successfully if you have clearly marshalled your thoughts beforehand. Far from finding the framework restricting, you will find it liberating.

I once worked on a documentary-style production for a Royal Shakespeare Company season at the Roundhouse. It was enormously exciting, because we could do anything; the script was a huge folder of items, and we could put the stage and the audience anywhere we liked in the huge, undefined space. We spent three weeks on improvisations of different ideas of staging (including a stage twenty feet wide and eighty feet long, dissecting the space, on to which the actors had to make each entrance running, so as to cover enough ground). All this was a complete waste of time, because until we had decided the ground rules – where the stage and audience were going to be, and what the form of the material was – we couldn't do any real work. Too much freedom can be a restriction!

## The moral

It is much better to change your mind about what you are writing at the planning stage, than to have to tackle rewriting a completed draft. That's not to say you won't want to modify your ideas as you go along. But if you work through your revisions in the storyline, the scene breakdown and the character and song plots before you write, you'll appreciate the implications, and know if the ideas for the new draft will work.

Before you start writing, you might find it interesting to examine the structure of a show you particularly like, and compare it with its original source material. See how it fits the rules and how it differs. It is also useful to do this if you've seen any of the recent clunkers and (knowing what you now know) try to define what went wrong.

# 4 Music

'I must say, Bernard Shaw is greatly improved by music.' That was T.S. Eliot's response to *My Fair Lady*. Music makes a very special contribution, and musicals are more often associated with the names of their composers than with those of their book or lyric writers. In the pop world it may suffice to hum a tune, supported by strumming a chord (from a repertoire of three), but composing for the theatre requires some basic musical knowledge, so as to create something interesting enough to sustain a whole evening of theatrical drama.

## Where to begin

In films, music is in the background, helping to create the mood. In musical theatre, music is in the foreground and is part of the action; mood setting, though important, is secondary. Music should play an important part in establishing character and purpose. It also helps to create the situation where the audience thinks or feels what you want it to, which is much harder than simply telling it what to think or feel.

Before you begin to write a number you and your collaborators must define precisely what you are trying to achieve. What sort of number is it? How does it sound? What does it do? Who is it for? Use your knowledge of existing songs to describe your intentions; for instance, is it a 'Flash Bang Wallop', or a 'Bring Him Home' type of number? The music must suit the title of the song, the particular character singing it and the time and place in which it is set. It should also support the lyric, so that the two are as one and do not compete for the attention of the audience (who must be able to hear the words clearly). If the response to the song is 'Nice tune, but I didn't understand the words', then the composer has failed just as much as the lyricist.

Having established within the whole writing team what the song has to do, and how it will do it, the composer and lyricist must come to an agreement as to what happens next. In most cases the lyricist produces a lyric for the composer to set; 'words first' has become more popular as lyrics have become more complex and important to the story-telling. Nevertheless, it all depends on the dynamics of the writing team. Andrew Lloyd Webber initiates his projects and always lays out the music first.

Character should be expressed in the music as well as the dialogue or lyrics. Each of the principal characters should have a number which offers them the opportunity to expound or display their character or philosophy. This must be done with great care, and properly integrated into the story – the show must not stop while they come forward to tell the audience about themselves. It should musically underline their character – be it the Latin rhythms of *Kiss of the Spider Woman*, or the stabbing, pointilliste notes of *Sunday in the Park with George* – and can then be used as their theme throughout the show. In *Merrily We Roll Along* Stephen Sondheim takes this to the ultimate, all the composer-hero's songs – 'The Hills of Tomorrow', 'Old Friends/Like It Was', 'Good Thing Going' and 'Our Time' – being developments of the same theme.

Contrast is vitally important in constructing a score. If a show is to have variety, you should look for opportunities for as many different sounds as possible – solos, duets, trios, quartets and concerted numbers (tutti). Male duets, which are very underrated, can be extremely powerful; 'You're Nothing Without Me', a duet between writer Stein and his creation Stone is a dynamic first-act closer in *City of Angels*. Likewise, within the overall stylistic framework you choose, you should employ as many different rhythms and types of number as your story-telling will allow. Songs of similar mood and tempo should not follow one another.

Counterpoint is literally note against note, or tune against tune: that is, two people singing different tunes at the same time. Probably the best known example is 'I Hear Music'/'You're Just In Love' from *Call Me Madam*, 'Side by Side'/'What Would We Do Without You?' from *Company* is another example. This can make very exciting theatre, offering the opportunity for a musical argument or conflict – two opposing characters pitting their philosophies against one another, for example, or a combative love relationship being established. The tunes must be contrasting in both tempo and note register, yet they must fit together. The main tune must be firmly established for the audience before the counter tune is added.

## Song types

### Ballads

These are the most common because of the emotional nature of musical theatre. They are melody-dominant and must be tuneful, since they are what the audience will remember. They should be smooth-flowing (*legato*) and tender. They are personal, suiting the moments when one character is yearning for another, or two characters find each other, or the soliloquy where a character examines his feelings. Examples are 'The Music Of The Night' in *The Phantom of The Opera*, and 'On My Own' from *Les Miserables*.

### Rhythm

These are rhythm-dominant. They must have a steady, rhythmic accompaniment and usually an optimistic or happy tone, with a more definite sense of movement. Examples are 'You Could Drive a Person Crazy' in *Company*, and 'I Got Rhythm' in *Crazy For You*. They are more public, and the full-company numbers are usually rhythm numbers.

## Comedy or Point

The main function of these numbers is to be funny. Music itself cannot do this, so it must simply serve the lyric – that is, point it up. Such numbers can be either private or public, solo or full-company. Examples are 'Adelaide's Lament' in *Guys and Dolls*, and 'Master of the House' in *Les Miserables*.

## Production Numbers

These are full-company numbers and are often used to introduce locations or relationships, or bring events to a public climax, most commonly in act-openers or -closers. They may be very up-front, as with 'Another Opening, Another Show' in *Kiss Me Kate*, or much more circumlocutory, as with 'Magic to Do' in *Pippin*. Production numbers are also used to denote major changes in plot or location, and in montages which compress time. They are usually rhythm numbers.

## Musical Scenes

It is common nowadays for songs to develop into scenes, being a mixture of sung and underscored spoken words. This is a technique that Stephen Sondheim uses a great deal for both comedy, as in 'You Must Meet My Wife' in *A Little Night Music*, and drama, as in 'Epiphany' in *Sweeney Todd*.

## Reprises

A reprise is a return to (not a repeat of) a song. While the lyrics often change, the music must not. The idea is to revisit in order to make a specific point. It must say something which a new song wouldn't be able to do. You may take a whole song to convey the idea, or you may be able to do it with just a fragment or phrase incorporated into another song; in *Jesus Christ Superstar*, Judas (showing remorse after the betrayal) sings only the words I DON'T

KNOW HOW TO LOVE HIM from Mary's song. Reprises can also be used as linking material in stories that involve major leaps in time or location. You can orientate the audience by employing them as markers. *Merrily We Roll Along* moves backwards in time over a period of twenty-five years. Whenever there is a time lapse, a reprise of the title number signals the change and counts off the years. Do not use reprises as just a cheap repeat of the tune so that the audience can go out whistling it.

## Setting lyrics

This is the moment when the gloves come off. There will inevitably be conflicts of interest between the demands of the lyric and the demands of the tune. Compromise is not easy and (what's worse) often not productive. This is the main reason why writing teams produce different songs for the same slot; matching exactly the right lyric with exactly the right tune isn't easy, or in some cases even possible. But what you must not do is accept second best.

Language has its own natural rhythm. The tune must respect this and not seek to impose an unnatural one. Spoken words naturally form themselves into rhythmic groups of two, three or four, and the tune must take account of this. There should be one beat per syllable, with the musical stress falling on the natural stress of the word as it would be spoken. The phrasing must allow the singer to breathe, and project the words in such a manner that the audience can understand him.

Changes in pitch accentuate the word, and the highest pitch should again be on the stressed beat. The highest notes in the tune will give importance to the words which fall on them; they should therefore be the most important word in the sense or title of the song, and not the 'ifs', 'ands' or 'buts'. The intervals between successive notes will also draw attention to the words, particularly if they are within one word. Octave jumps can be used to create emotion and drama.

## Song form

The root of most western popular music is the form of four blocks of the same length, usually eight bars, making songs generally thirty-two bars overall. There are three main expressions of this form. Note that these refer to *form*, and not rhyme scheme.

### Popular Song Form (AABA)

**A:**  the main melodic theme
**A:**  the same theme repeated
**B:**  a contrasting melody (the bridge or release)
**A:**  the main theme repeated to bring the song to resolution

This is the form of most popular songs. The advantage for the theatre is that the main theme is heard three times, which plants it in the audience's memory. The second **A** should modulate (move towards another key) so that there will be some melodic and harmonic variation in the **B** section. This contrast can also be achieved by different note values (making the tempo feel different, even though it is the same) or a different time signature. In order for the number to build there should be a further modulation for the last **A** section. Although the song is thirty-two bars long, you are only writing sixteen bars of music. Songs in this form include 'Tomorrow' from *Annie*, 'Memory' from *Cats*, and 'The Best of Times' from *La Cage aux Folles*.

### Show Tune Form (ABAC)

**A:**  the main melodic theme
**B:**  a contrasting melody
**A:**  the main theme repeated
**C:**  a developed theme to bring the song to resolution

This offers you the opportunity for the resolution to be more climactic, while still allowing the audience to hear the main theme twice. Here, although the song is thirty-two bars long, you are only writing twenty-four bars of music. Songs in this form include: 'Hello Dolly' from *Hello Dolly*, 'If They Could See Me Now' from *Sweet Charity*, and 'But Not For Me' from *Crazy for You*.

## Verse Chorus Form (ABAB)

**A:**  the main melodic theme
**B:**  a contrasting melody
**A:**  the main theme repeated
**B:**  the contrasting theme repeated

The repetitive nature of this form means that it is more suitable for comedy songs, with a different and strong punchline in the lyric at the end of each chorus. Again, although the song is thirty-two bars long, you are only writing sixteen bars of music. A good example of crafting a number in this form is in *Me and My Girl*, where 'The Lambeth Walk' was built into a show-stopping first-act finale. It is simply two eight-bar blocks, repeated seven times, but it moves skilfully from solos to a small group, to spoon playing, to dance, and finally to the whole company singing and dancing, as the tempo increases and the key modulates. Other songs in this form include 'There is Nothing Like a Dame' from *South Pacific*, and 'Gee, Officer Krupke' from *West Side Story*.

## Variations

Sometimes the thirty-two bar form has been either expanded or contracted by writers who found that it did not meet their needs. An **AABAA** form was used for 'Send in the Clowns' in *A Little Night Music*. Rather more common is the **ABA** form used for 'Wilkommen' in *Cabaret*, and 'Bidin' My Time' in *Crazy For You*.

The basic form may be preceded by an introductory section to set up the number – often posing a question to which the main song is the answer. These introductions can be any length, and have varied from one line for 'Johnny One-Note' from *Babes in Arms* to seventeen lines for 'I'll Know' from *Guys and Dolls*. You must take care that the introduction is not so long (or so good) that it outshines the actual song it is supposed to be introducing. In recent years, the sung introduction has frequently been replaced by underscoring, as a more subtle way of blending the change from speech to song.

Sometimes there may be an interlude within a number – for either a dance section or underscored dialogue – but it does not count as part of the thirty-two bars. There may also be a four-bar extension to the final section, to provide a more definite resolution by repeating the last two lines. It is not uncommon in fast-moving songs for the length of the blocks to be doubled to sixteen bars, making a total of sixty-four bars.

Each block of eight bars has traditionally been broken down into four equal two-bar phrases or lines. In recent years alternative breakdowns, such as five and three, have been successfully employed.

It may seem restrictive to work to song forms like these, but – as with the show as a whole – you will find it is actually a great help to have a framework to work to. It will enable you to avoid the formless sprawl which many new writers produce. Through-written shows have, in most cases, ignored such a framework at their peril – with all manner of bits and pieces, tacked on here and there, unfocussing the score.

## Rhythm

Rhythm should be used to provide a sense of propulsion to the music, even in ballads. It should be combined with progressive harmonies to provide a feeling of movement. Rhythm is the defining element in a song; any melody set to a different rhythm turns into a different song without changing a note. A good example of this was in *Maria Friedman By Special Arrangement*, when the band played 'The Blue Danube' as a samba (particularly the chorus which just used percussion).

Rhythm is written down as a time signature, indicating the number of beats in a bar. The two basic time signatures of show music are 2/4 and 3/4, everything else being multiples of them.

> *2/4* (up tempo) is fast and lively, with two beats to the bar. It feels the most rhythmic because every other downbeat is an accent: **1** 2, **1** 2, **1** 2, **1** 2.
> *3/4* (waltz) is flowing and lilting, with three beats to the bar: **1** 2 3, **1** 2 3, **1** 2 3, **1** 2 3.
> *4/4* (common time) is slow and easy, with four beats to the bar. It has the main accent on the downbeat, and a secondary accent on the third beat: **1** 2 3 4, **1** 2 3 4, **1** 2 3 4, **1** 2 3 4.

Syncopation is the accenting of a beat which is not the main accented beat in a bar. Often this is the third beat in 4/4 time. It was used effectively in 'I Can See It' in *The Fantasticks*.

More esoteric forms from 5/4 through 6/8 to 2/8 are not unknown. Andrew Lloyd Webber has often used 5/4, from 'Everything's All Right' in *Jesus Christ Superstar* onwards. 'Let's Do Lunch' in *Sunset Boulevard* has different rhythms for each section and boasts no time signature as such.

## Musical elements

The musical elements are interdependent and are used in the creation of all songs regardless of style or type.

*Melody* is a succession of notes that has a recognizable shape. There are two main ingredients: repetition – the same phrase repeated, and travel – the range of notes encompassed and the relationship of the first with the last. The melody should be as 'rememberable' as possible. Often the simplest tune, with only a modest range, is the easiest to remember – hence the best ones have been written for singers of limited range. The melody should indicate the character or situation of the performer.

*Harmony* is the simultaneous sounding of different notes

in a way that is musically significant. Melody has natural harmonic implications. Harmony creates tension with the tune to generate a feeling of pushing ahead. Endeavour to avoid the original key and dominant harmony until the obvious resolution at the end of the song. Bear possible harmonies in mind when you are writing duets, trios, quartets and tuttis.

*A Chord* is any combination of three or more notes played simultaneously. In western music, chords are constructed from the seven different notes of the scale (Do–Re–Me–Fa–Sol–La–Ti) used alternately. The more notes that are used, the more complex the chord, thus:

| | |
|---|---|
| Triads | Do–Me–Sol |
| 7ths | Do–Me–Sol–Ti |
| 9ths | Do–Me–Sol–Ti–Re |
| 11ths | Do–Me–Sol–Ti–Re–Fa |
| 13ths | Do–Me–Sol–Ti–Re–Fa–La |

*Modulation* is lifting the key up by a half-tone, usually when moving into or out of the bridge, or for the final block. This gives a sense of momentum and can be combined with an actual increase in tempo to drive numbers on. Whole-tone modulation can also be used, and modulation downwards is possible, but less usual. Common-tone modulation means taking the last note of one block as the starting point for the next.

*Keys* have their own 'colour'. Consequently, the key in which a tune is played affects the way it sounds; in some circumstances the difference between one key and another can be quite radical. When you are composing you should choose whichever key sounds best (even if, like Irving Berlin, you can only play in one key and have to buy a piano which changes it for you). Be prepared for a song to be transposed (changed to a different key from that in which it was written) during rehearsals, so that the actor can be comfortable singing it in eight shows a week. The musical director must be certain that this will not adversely affect how it will sound.

*Mood* should be evoked by the style of the music

supporting the sense and meaning of the lyric. From around the mid-eighteenth century (largely under the influence of Gluck) it was decided that all happy songs should be in major keys and all sad songs in minor ones. In recent years composers have begun to break out of this straitjacket, and it is no longer obligatory.

*Tempo* should not be confused with rhythm. The tempo is the speed at which the counts of the rhythm are played. You can have 3/4 played faster than 2/4. While interpretations of a tempo can vary from conductor to conductor, it can be fixed with complete accuracy by the use of a metronome. It can then be logged as a number on the music. This may be necessary when synchronizing with a pre-recorded vocal or music track to avoid a gear-change. Music tracks are used a good deal in *The Phantom of the Opera*. The tell-tale sign is if the musical director is wearing headphones.

The *Hook* is a repeated or clever phrase in the lyric which will imprint on the audience's brain. You should find a musical equivalent. Tunes need to be engineered so that they are easily remembered.

*Style* is something that all writers have, whether they are aware of it or not. It is largely dictated by their personal likes and dislikes. You may not have analysed precisely what it is about your favourite music that appeals to you, but there will be certain keys, tones, harmonic and melodic combinations that you like, just as there are individual qualities in people that you find attractive. When you compose, these likes and dislikes will subconsciously govern what you produce. You must make sure that your voice does not conflict with the voice of your story, or that of your characters.

## Voice: the principal instrument

In a production, your music may be arranged for a single piano or a symphony orchestra. However, whatever the instruments are, they will be supporting a human voice. You need to know the range of the instruments when you come to consider the orchestration, but from the outset of your writing you must keep one particular instrument in mind: the human voice.

It is no use producing the best score in the world if it is unsingable, or a role is uncastable. It's not a bad idea to write with 'wish-list' casting in mind, to focus your work, but don't write something that only one person can sing – because you are scuppered if they can't (or won't). Most singers have a range of about one and a half octaves, or twelve notes; two octaves is exceptional. Most songs therefore have a range of about ten notes.

The general female ranges are:

| | |
|---|---|
| Soprano: | Middle C to A below Top C |
| Mezzo: | A below Middle C to G below Top C |
| Alto: | G below Middle C to A above Middle C |

and the general male ranges are:

| | |
|---|---|
| Tenor: | C below Middle C to A above Middle C |
| Baritone: | A twice below Middle C to E above Middle C |
| Bass: | G twice below Middle C to Middle C |

The colour, or timbre, of a voice also changes how we perceive the sound; the same note will sound lower when sung by a dark voice than when by a bright one, in the same way that the key in which the note is written will affect how it sounds.

Singers actually have two voices – head voice and chest voice – the difference being where the sound resonates. The higher part of their register is focused in their head, and the lower in their chest. Each produces a different quality of sound. The head voice is a lyrical, tender and more vulnerable sound, needed for ballads. The chest voice (known as belting) is more knowing and aggressive, suitable for rhythm or comedy songs.

At some point there is a gear-change from one voice to the other. This is something that all singers try to make as smooth as possible, but it cannot be eliminated. At auditions the musical director will need to ensure that this break does not occur at an important or exposed point in your songs. Exceptional voices can stretch the rules. Elaine Paige is a soprano who can produce notes in her upper range from her chest voice – and Mandy Patinkin is a man, who though nominally a tenor, can sing soprano – but it would be best not to write with such demands in mind. The hyper-emotional style of writing employed by Boublil and Schonberg in *Les Miserables, Miss Saigon* and *Martin Guerre* tends to require a particular sort of head belt: a gut-wrenching scream at the top of the singer's range. This puts heavy demands on the voice and means that, as in opera, actors are often unable to perform eight shows a week.

There is a wide gulf between opera and musical theatre singers, because of their training. Opera singers are encouraged to pursue musical tone at the expense of the meaning and clarity of the words – which is why they generally make a mess of musicals, which require the reverse priority. Sometimes it is difficult to tell if an opera is being sung in English or the original language. (It is amazing that people complain of not being able to hear the words of pop songs, when opera is often worse.)

## The dots

Most composers work with their collaborators by putting their work down on tape. For themselves, and when they need to communicate their ideas to the world at large, they will need to commit them to paper.

### The Lead Sheet

The lead sheet is the composer's equivalent of a script. It is the basic tool to convey his intentions to the creative team (see Figure 6). It must therefore be specific and should contain:

*The Melody* – with the time signature and key signature clearly marked.

*The Harmony* – with the chords marked in musical symbols over the appropriate places.

*The Lyrics* – with each syllable spaced directly under the note on which it is sung.

*The Style* – a description of the way in which it should be played, either formal (e.g. *prestissimo*) or informal (e.g. manic/fast).

**Figure 6    A Lead Sheet**

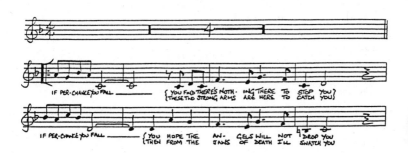

## The Piano Vocal Score

When a show moves into production the lead sheet will no longer be detailed enough to ensure that the performance remains true to your original concept, and does not become something else. It must evolve – with assistance from an arranger or supervisor, if necessary – into the Piano Vocal Score. It is this that will form the audition and rehearsal parts for pianists and performers, and on which the musical director and orchestrator will base their work. It defines more clearly how the final result will sound (see Figure 7).

## Music only

There will be a number of points in the score when you will use music only, without lyrics.

## Figure 7   A Piano Vocal Score

## Dance

The most important use of music without words is dance. The days of the dream ballet are past, and, sadly, shows nowadays tend to have a lower dance content than they used to. Nevertheless dance is an important part of musical theatre, and you are missing an opportunity if you don't explore its possibilities. You won't be able to write a dance sequence at the outset, in the same way that you can write dialogue or lyrics. As you develop the show, however, you can add variety and inventiveness by creating opportunities for dance or movement to be the major part of the story-telling process. Musically you will be able to write a sketch for a sequence, which you will later be able to develop with the choreographer, and finalize with the dancers in rehearsal.

## Incidental (Linking and Scene Changes)

However a show is physically staged and scene changes are handled – whether by blackouts, scene changes in view, or a bare stage where an actor simply moves to a different area – there will be a need for music to punctuate the action. Your aim must be to link one scene with the next and to prepare the audience for what is to come. This is an important function, and can make a big difference to how an audience receives a show.

Since contrast is an essential part of the construction of a musical, music must provide lubrication for the gear-changes. The audience must be brought down from a comic high point and put into a mood for listening to the drama that follows. Conversely, they must be eased out of the pain of one event and into the knockabout scene which follows. You can trigger the mood changes by the use of character themes and reprised material, with arrangements that indicate location and time of day.

Once the score is complete you should take the artistic decisions as to what the incidental music will consist of. It may seem unimportant, but it isn't. When you get to the band calls you will be surprised just how large a percentage of the score this material comprises. The precise length of piece you will need for each link will not be known until the set is up and working, and the transformation has been staged. It should incorporate some sort of repeat to make it open-ended enough to cope with unforeseen circumstances.

## Underscoring

Underscoring is music that is played 'under' dialogue. It can be used in various ways. In a dialogue scene it can add weight by pointing or counterpointing the words and heightening their impact. Linked songs can be joined together, spanning the scene that separates them. Numbers now often start with, or incorporate, dialogue sections that are underscored.

Generally underscoring is reprised or preprised material and not something written in its own right. This gives it a quality of association that adds something to the dialogue. Usually it consists of only part of a number, and may include phrases from different songs, possibly employing character themes. This technique, much used by Andrew

Lloyd Webber and his orchestrator, allows tunes to be planted or reinforced in the mind of the audience. Just to prove that there is nothing new, however: it was used by Jerome Kern in *Showboat*, where the theme of 'Old Man River' appears in the opening number.

As you create the piece, you should formulate ideas about what you can use for underscoring, and where. Final details will have to wait until rehearsals, when you can dovetail speech and action with music. You should think of underscoring as salt or spice. Don't douse the entire show in it for its own sake; it must be artistically valid.

## Overture, Entr'acte, Curtain Calls and Play-out

These are vital elements that are often not given enough attention. The overture introduces the audience to the world into which they are being invited, and it should metaphorically be the show in headlines, enticing them to want to hear more. Usually made up of the main theme of the show interpolated with other strong numbers, it is the countdown to a successful lift-off. The entr'acte has to re-acquaint the audience with where the show left off before the interval and take them forward, proving that it hasn't run out of steam. It is normally about half the length of the overture. The curtain calls should recapitulate the whole show, to remind the audience what a wonderful piece of theatre you have created. The play-out must send them out into the night singing the songs, and dying to ring up their friends to tell them what a great night out they have had.

These pieces are always finalized at the last minute, to avoid the costly problem of re-orchestration if any of the numbers they contain should be cut. Nevertheless, they should be planned well in advance to achieve maximum effect, and then modified as necessary.

## The music department

Traditionally, shows used to have both an orchestrator and

an arranger (sometimes two of them, with one concentrating on the dance sequences). Today the arranger has all but disappeared, and his role often merged with that of the orchestrator, or with the newer position of musical supervisor.

## Arranger

In the palmy days, the arranger took the lead sheets from the composer and crafted the final versions of the songs as used in the show, producing the piano vocal score. It was he who was responsible for creating the linking, underscoring and dance music in collaboration with the director and choreographer. Arrangers often added a necessary element of musicianship to very basic ideas that often came from the composer as no more than a melody line. Everyone involved had a far more cavalier attitude to creating musicals than they do today. Now, writers are more involved in the finer details of what happens to their work and, if capable, do much of the arranger's job themselves. The increasing complexity and quality of the lyricist's work has been matched by the greater musical knowledge and expertise of composers.

## Musical Supervisor

In recent years the role of Musical Supervisor has been created as overall head of the music department. The musical supervisor provides musical expertise, as arrangers once did, ensures that the composer's intentions are clearly conveyed to the orchestrator and musical director, and co-ordinates all the musical elements. Once the show has been successfully launched, he travels the world overseeing the franchised productions.

## Orchestrator

Working from the piano vocal score and other information gleaned from detailed discussions with the composer, arranger and/or musical supervisor, the orchestrator

## Figure 8   A Conductor's Score

writes the notes that each individual musician will play (see Figure 8 for an example of a full orchestration from a conductor's score). The overall sound which you wish to create, be it 1940s big band for *City of Angels*, or contemporary electronic for *Company*, will (together with the producer's budget) dictate the musical line-up. In the days of Rodgers and Hammerstein, orchestras of thirty-six were common, but economics have determined that twenty is now considered lavish. It is the orchestrator's task to paint the musical picture that will support the performers and realize the composer's vision. The importance of his contribution is readily recognized by major composers. Stephen Sondheim always works with Jonathan Tunick, and Andrew Lloyd Webber with David Cullen.

The orchestrator has an awesome task, writing perhaps three thousand bars of music for six, twelve or even twenty-four people. Most of this will have to be done during the rehearsal period, since the final form of the material will not be decided until then. It is usual for orchestrators to attend a run-through to ensure what they are doing will fit with the staging. Orchestrations are like lighting, they are only noticed when they are not working properly.

## Copyists

As the orchestrator finishes his work, it is passed to copyists who will write out a conductor's score, with all the parts in, and an individual pad for each musician's stand. It is not unknown for this process to get so far behind, that copyists are working around the clock in rooms adjacent to the rehearsals. Parts can be rushed to band calls with the ink still wet. No major production has yet had sufficient faith to rely entirely on a computer for its orchestrating and copying.

## Musical Director

The Musical Director is the person in charge of the music

on a nightly basis. He will conduct in performance, and he is responsible for maintaining musical standards both in the pit and on the stage. At the auditions, the MD will ensure that the artists will be able to deal with the musical challenges which you have set them. In rehearsal, working with the arranger or supervisor, he will decide what harmonies will be sung, set the keys and teach the music to the performers. In consultation with the director and choreographer, he will refine the shape of the numbers and set the tempi. At the band calls he will take the musicians through the music, ensuring that the work he has done in rehearsal coalesces with what is written on the stave.

### Fixer

The Fixer (with all its mafia overtones) is the common name for the Orchestral Manager. He is sub-contracted by the producer to find, organize and discipline the musicians, fulfilling the role of a pair of rubber gloves, so that the creative team do not have to soil themselves by dealing with musicians direct. Often fixers are players themselves, and may be playing in one show while managing two or three others. This can lead to problems, if they are not on the spot to deal with emergencies. A West End show had to be cancelled on a Saturday night because of a communication breakdown. Before the era of mobile phones, pagers were used by fixers to keep in touch, and when the MD sent the panic message: 'Ring theatre – no drummer', this unfortunately came out as 'Ring theatre – no drama', so the fixer didn't call until the interval – by which time it was too late.

### The Musicians

Finally we reach the pits. Everything you have ever heard about musicians or 'musos' is true, except that the most outrageous things are probably an understatement. At the interval they *are* out of the pit and rocketing pubwards through the stage door (stopwatch in hand) by the time the house lights are up. The reason they stare at their music stands so intently is because they *are* reading pornographic magazines. (The MD, since he is facing in the opposite direction and the audience can see over his shoulder, has to make do with innocuous material like the *Radio Times*.) They *truly* neither know nor care what is happening on stage. There *are* nights when three-quarters of them are deputies who have never played it before. On the anniversary of a show I worked on, the composer (who currently has shows running all over the world) conducted the playout in a less than proficient manner. The fixer immediately came round to complain, threatening that if he ever did that again, next time they would follow him – with obviously disastrous consequences.

# 5   Lyrics

At a social gathering someone remarked to Mrs Richard Rodgers, 'So your husband wrote "Some Enchanted Evening" ' – at which Mrs Oscar Hammerstein interrupted, 'No, *my* husband wrote "Some Enchanted Evening". *Her* husband only wrote "la-da da-da de de".' Lyricists tend to get the blame for a poor song, while composers get the credit for a good one.

## The short end of the baton

Don't be a lyricist. In the three-way relationship between composer, book writer and lyricist you're the piggy in the middle, the gooseberry at the party. You get the worst billing, and, if the critics don't like the music, you'll get slammed or ignored.

You also have to do the most work. The composer writes sixteen bars of music and he's through. You have to write thirty-two bars' worth of lyrics – all different, all rhyming and all saying something interesting. On top of that, if the song is cut or the show is never produced, the composer has a tune for his bottom drawer, but all you have is a lyric for the bin. Alan Jay Lerner joked about the lyricist locked in a hotel room for three days working on a song. Asked what he has been writing he replies; 'I could have danced all night. I could have danced all night, and still have begged for more'. The writer is carted off by men in white jackets and put away.

There is an up-side of course. It's the songs that

audiences remember. When a lyric successfully captures the feeling and the moment, it is the essence of musical theatre. It defines the musical.

## Lyric expression

Music sets the mood for a song, while the lyric imparts the specific idea and tells the story. It defines what the singer is thinking and feeling. Lyrics must be the method by which a character *expresses* feelings, rather than describes them. *Out of the Blue,* a musical about the bombing of Hiroshima, failed to work for many reasons, but the principal one was that the audience didn't *see* anything actually happen. The characters told each other about things that had happened, but they didn't actually experience things, with the audience eavesdropping as they did so.

Stephen Sondheim said: 'Not enough songwriters understand the function of the song in a play. They write songs in which a character explains himself – this is self-defeating because the song should reveal the character to the audience; the character doesn't have the self-knowledge. We do, he doesn't. That's the problem in most shows: characters coming out and singing about their drives, but there are so many other ways to tell a story'.

## What is a lyric?

Lyrics are more difficult to write than dialogue because they are more compressed, in the same way that dialogue is more compressed than real speech. Thus song is the next stage on from the carefully polished phrase or the well-crafted gag. It, too, is carefully polished and well-crafted, but it is also rhymed, and set to music. Music and lyrics totalled together must add up to *more* than the sum of the parts. Dialogue can make a dramatic statement in three words 'I love you' or 'I hate you'. Lyrics qualify or amplify this basic statement, and how they do so must be worth the time spent doing it. Beaumarchais' remark that 'if something is not worth saying, people sing it' referred to opera; it does not apply to musical theatre.

Almost the most important thing to learn is that lyrics are not poetry set to music. Attempts to do this generally fail, because they detract from the words, rather than adding to them. The most successful efforts have taken John Betjeman's work and underscored it (providing mood and ambience) rather than actually setting it to music in the conventional sense. Poetry is meant to be read; lyrics are meant to be heard with music, and they are incomplete without it. Their meaning must be immediately and fully understood by an audience at the first hearing, with no recap. Poetry should reveal greater depths the more it is studied, but lyrics that require study inevitably fail. Once an audience stops to wonder what something meant, you have lost them.

Like poetry, however, good lyric writing demands the avoidance of unnecessary or redundant words. Economy is important. Most lyrics contain less than 150 words, so each one must count; ideas must be expressed simply and briefly (it's not what you put in, it's what you leave out). You must find images and rhymes that are fresh and not clichés, and new situations to use them in. Images must be organized, and should not leap off confusingly in all directions at once. What you should aim for is clarity. Lyrics will only be heard, so you must avoid any possible ambiguities from words that sound alike. (Did you mean 'to', 'two' or 'too'?)

In poetry, writers aim for the number of syllables to be uniform, while in lyrics it should be as varied as possible within the regular two-bar phrase, and the nature of the music (that is, the number of notes within the bars) will affect the number of words. Use polysyllabic words with restraint, however, unless you are making a particular point about a character; monosyllabic words are easier to comprehend. Also, lyrics should have the natural speech rhythms of Shakespeare or Molière and should not sound like nursery-rhyme doggerel. Don't make a stop at the end of each line, but carry the thought around the end of the line and complete it somewhere in the next one.

As musical theatre and pop songs have diverged, the quality of musical-theatre lyrics has risen, while that of pop lyrics has deteriorated. Show songs have become more specific, and so less likely to have a future outside the theatre. People still feel pressure to attempt to write a hit song in order to sell the show, but you will fail if you make this your priority. Look on any song you write as a ticket in a lottery. Remember that hundreds of songs fail to win every day, without having to fit into a musical as well. Stick to the job in hand; it's hard enough in itself.

It is a common failing for new writers to think that something is a 'good idea' without having anything to say. The idea for a lyric must be big enough to support a whole song. It must not be exhausted by the end of the first four bars, so that you have to find seven more ways of saying the same thing. There should be a title song, since it will help to sell the show, but it must be a good song with a strong idea. It must earn its place, and not be there just because you are required to write one. 'Hello Dolly' makes the show, while 'Kiss Me Kate' smacks of coercion.

As with writing the scenes, you should write the numbers with an idea of staging possibilities in mind. You need to think in three dimensions. An entire evening of performers standing downstage centre, singing straight out to the audience, will be tedious, no matter how good the lyrics are.

## Lyric content

The lyric content is what the song says. It is defined by a number of factors.

*Purpose.* Every song must have a specific purpose – to change a character's mind about an action, to reveal an unknown truth, to resolve a confrontation. By the end of the song the situation must have changed. Show songs make a difference.

*Topic.* The topic of the song may be seemingly unrelated

to the subject (from which a moral or conclusion may be drawn) because it is more interesting for an audience to receive information in an oblique way than an obvious one.

*Vocabulary*. It is important that people should not step out of character when they sing. Their use of language, and the sentiments that the characters express, should be at one with the dialogue. The lyric must therefore reflect their period, class and education. Characters must speak with their own voice (not that of the lyricist), and images used in the lyric should come from their world. How they express themselves is as revealing to an audience as what they say. Stephen Sondheim says that he now regrets in *West Side Story*, Maria's line IT'S ALARMING HOW CHARMING I FEEL, because it is too sophisticated. He also says that the line I FEEL FIZZY AND FUNNY AND FINE is a good example of a lyricist with nothing much to say. Both dialogue and lyrics must serve the character, not display the talent of the writer. If they don't, the character loses credibility with the audience.

*Character*: The nature of the character singing the lyric will affect how the topic is presented, and how the purpose is fulfilled. It will be revealed by the lyric, but it should not be stated overtly. Thus, in *Company*, the purpose of Joanne's song 'Ladies Who Lunch' is to reveal the emptiness of her life; the topic is defined by the title, she is the subject, and her character is underlined by the point of view she expounds.

## Song Types

The musical differences between song types that have already been discussed are reflected in their lyrics, and to some extent determine the nature of the lyric.

### Ballads

Ballads are generally reflective, telling you more about the characters. Usually the songs that make the show, they are the sweeping emotional statements which everyone remembers. The biggest problem is that it has all been said before; greater talents than yours have been defeated by trying to write yet another song that simply says 'I love you'. (According to the Performing Rights Society there are already 1,424 with those words for a title, never mind all the others that include the same sentiment.) The challenge is to find a new and interesting angle for the song. Your inspiration should come from making it intensely personal – so that it springs from the particular character or characters singing it, and the situation in which they find themselves. After all, every relationship in real life is unique. In gentler times Oscar Hammerstein often put a twist on situations by using flirting: for instance with 'If I Loved You' in *Carousel*, and 'Only Make Believe' in *Showboat*.

Slow music requires short thoughts. Long sentences are so drawn out that the ear loses track of the meaning. If possible, the thoughts need to be contained within a single two-bar phrase.

## Rhythm

Rhythm songs are, by their nature, more extrovert, and they tend to provide the character and concerted or full company numbers. They are usually active – advancing the plot – and form the opening and closing numbers of each act. Since they will introduce new information, or dramatize conflict, they will be more straightforward in approach and offer less opportunity for imagery. They can stem from more quirky and unusual ideas than ballads.

## Comedy or Point

A comedy song cannot be a joke set to music; it must arise from the situation and the character singing it. You cannot sit through the whole song for a punchline at the end. The comedy should be experience-related and highly personal. It can be very effective if the character singing the song is deadly serious, and the comedy comes from how reality differs from his expectation.

Just as in telling a joke, the material must be carefully organized. There should be a strong rhyme scheme, which will encourage the audience to predict the joke. This gives you the opportunity either to confirm their anticipation or to confound it and pull the rug from under them. There must be a set-up, a development and a pay-off. The last line is most important, so you should start there and work backwards. The most successful form is to aim for short jokes and to have a complete joke in each block – making four separate punch lines in all. Each one must be stronger than its predecessor, with the best saved for last. You can try one long joke, with the pay-off in the last line but, if you do, the pay-off must relate to (and build on) mini-jokes in the other blocks, and the idea must be a very strong one to sustain such length.

## *Laundry List or Catalogue Songs*

In these, the lyric is mostly made up of lists of items. They can be serious, like 'The Impossible Dream' from *Man of La Mancha*, but are most frequently comic, like 'The Little Things You Do Together' in *Company*. This is a tempting style of song to choose, because it looks easy. It isn't; a list *per se* is not of any interest to your audience. You get no marks just for mentioning things. What makes it work are:

Unusual or unlikely juxtapositions.
Particularly clever or witty rhymes and presentation.
Defying the audience's expectation.
A sensationally clever and unexpected finish.

Unless you can meet all these criteria do not attempt it. 'Brush Up Your Shakespeare' in *Kiss Me Kate* is a good example, which works because unlikely characters are singing it, and yet it is their very background that provides the punch line.

## Titles

Titles are difficult to get right, since they must be a

summation of what the song is about, defining both situation and subject. The title can be the point of departure: the reason for the song exploring an idea. Alternatively, it can be the place of arrival: the conclusion which the song reaches. It should be as succinct as possible and, like a newspaper headline, must sell the song. The longest ever title (by Oscar Hammerstein) is 'Do I Love You Because You're Beautiful, Or Are You Beautiful Because I Love You?' Surprisingly, it was used in the lyric only once.

Since the title will affect how the song is perceived you must beware of irony. It may be too subtle for your audience and mislead them, so that they misinterpret what you are saying. One show I was involved with had a number singled out by a critic as being completely out of character. He had seen the title and, having already formed an opinion, had not listened carefully to the lyrics.

In an **AABA** song, the title should be in the first **A**, usually in the first or last line. It may be in the second **A** in an amended form, and must be in the last **A** in its original form. Thus it will have been heard three times. If it is the last line, it usually only rhymes in the final section to form the resolution. It will not be in the **B** which will explore the idea in a different way. In an **ABAC** song the title should also appear in the **C**. In an **ABAB** song the title should be in the **B**, since it must be what the chorus is about. It cannot be in the introduction, if there is one.

Where the title is placed within the lyric determines what sort of number it is. If it is in the first line, the song will be more obvious, such as 'Hello Dolly' or 'I Am What I Am' from *La Cage aux Folles*. If it is in the last line, the song will be more lyrical and subtle, as in 'All I Ask of You' from *The Phantom of the Opera* or 'Wouldn't It Be Luverly?' from *My Fair Lady*. Comedy songs also use the title at the end, as a punchline – for example 'Doin' What Comes Natur'lly' from *Annie Get Your Gun* or 'You Can Always Count On Me' from *City of Angels*.

Wherever it is placed, the audience must be left in no doubt as to what the title is.

## Lyric structure

The lyric structure is how a song says something or conveys its message. Oscar Hammerstein said that a song should be constructed like a one act play – that is, with Exposition, Development and Resolution. Relating this to basic song form (**AABA**) the first two blocks, (being musically and lyrically of the same form) are the exposition, the third block (being different musically, lyrically and in thought) is the development, and the fourth block (which musically and lyrically repeats the first) is the resolution. This has been variously summarized as:

| | | |
|---|---|---|
| **A** | This what I believe | I think |
| **A** | Because | I think |
| **B** | But | Because |
| **A** | Why | It is |

Although the form of the lyrics is the same in all the **A** sections, they cannot simply be a repeat, as in a pop song. Each must have fresh ideas and images building on the previous ones. You should endeavour to contain one complete thought in each block.

The hook of a song is the lyrical or musical idea which grabs the listener's attention, and is usually contained within a key repetitive phrase in the **A** section, often forming the last or title line. It is at its most effective if the last line of the song has a particular punch. For instance, if it adds new meaning to what has gone before, springs a surprise, or reveals the song to have a different meaning from the one that the audience has inferred. In 'Guess Who I Saw Today?' a wife relates to her husband her afternoon shopping, ending in a cafe where she sees a couple obviously in love. The last line is GUESS WHO I SAW TODAY? I SAW YOU!

## Rhyme

A song is like a fireworks picture. It needs structure and

support. Lyrics are words fashioned into a particular shape; song form provides the framework which supports them, and it is rhyme that ties them to the structure. (The singer then lights the blue touch paper.) Rhymes should help the audience to understand the sense of the lyrics, and convey the ideas behind the song. To do this successfully, the rhyme should not accommodate the thought grudgingly, but leap ahead smoothing a path. Like good PR it should enhance the idea's reception by the panache of its presentation, rather than trying to present second-hand ideas as new, like bad PR.

Rhyme is matching the sounds of stressed syllables at the end of a line. A good rhyme is unexpected, and invests words with fresh meaning. It builds up an expectation in the audience, which it then satisfies by exceeding it. A poor rhyme will be predictable and will leave the audience bored, waiting with unsurprised resignation for its suspicions to be confirmed. There should be a variety of different sorts of rhymes within a lyric to give variety.

The meaning of the lyric is more important than the rhyme. The audience should remember the thought, and if the rhyme is too noticeable you have not succeeded. The age is over for the ultra-tricksy Cole Porter lyric, where the rhyme or alliteration is the whole point of the song, as in 'It's D-lovely' and 'Anything Goes'. You should aim for natural speech rhythms that just happen to fall into a clever rhyme; remember that complex rhyming implies education, so the level of sophistication should be dictated by the character who is singing.

## Rhyme Scheme

This is the pattern of rhyming within the eight-bar blocks referred to in discussing song form in the previous chapter (**AABA, ABAC** and **ABAB**). Each of the eight-bar blocks breaks down into four bar phrases or lines. There are three main rhyme schemes.

*Basic*, which rhymes the second and fourth lines:

a
b
c
b

*Couplet,* which rhymes the first and second lines, then the third and fourth lines:

a
a
b
b

*Alternating,* which rhymes the first and third lines, then the second and fourth lines:

a
b
a
b

All the blocks of a song will share the same rhyme scheme, although the actual sounds of the rhymes may be different in each block.

| Section | A | Rhyme scheme | | Rhyme sound | |
|---|---|---|---|---|---|
| | | | a | | a |
| | | | b | | b |
| | | | c | | c |
| | | | b | | b |
| Section | A | Rhyme scheme | a | Rhyme sound | d |
| | | | b | | e |
| | | | c | | f |
| | | | b | | e |
| Section | A | Rhyme scheme | a | Rhyme sound | g |
| | | | b | | h |
| | | | c | | i |
| | | | b | | h |

The **B** (and **C**) blocks of a song should change to a different rhyme scheme to provide maximum variation.

## *Forms and Types*

There are many forms of rhyme, depending on where the accent falls within the word or words:

| | |
|---|---|
| One-rhyme: | THING |
| Two-rhyme: | LING*ER* |
| Three-rhyme: | SING-*A-LONG* |
| Four-rhyme: | FING*ER OF FATE* |

Really entertaining rhymes come from inspiration, rather than from rhyming dictionaries. Here are a number of types you should explore:

*Internal* rhymes are rhymes within a line, as well as at the end of it:
NOW LIFE IS AS QUIET AS THE AVERAGE RIOT
AND THE SIGNS ARE THIS STRANGER SPELLS DANGER.
*Neologisms* are new or made-up words, or new uses of existing words or phrases. They must spring from the character, however, like a malapropism, and not just be a cheap trick:
ABSOBALLYLUTELY
HOW D'YER DO/CONTEMPLATE THE VIEW
*Apocopated* rhymes use only the first part of one of the words making the rhyme:
MUST/SUST(AIN)
*Mosaic* rhymes use two or more words to rhyme with one:
SIGHTS YOU'LL/DELIGHTFUL
*Implied* rhymes have a strong set-up, but they omit the actual rhyming word and leave it for the audience fill in. They are usually both comic and rude:
NOW YOU'RE STUCK/DON'T SAY ...
*Dropped* rhymes have a similar set-up, but the character dodges the completion with an aside.

In show songs rhymes must be perfect. These are rhymes in which vowel sounds, consonants and stresses echo each other exactly; that is, matching syllables beginning with different letters: BACK/CRACK or PANE/RAIN.

Imperfect rhymes are similar but not exact: BACK/ CRACKED or PANE/RAINS. For instance, you should not use:

| | |
|---|---|
| paper rhymes: | LOOK/SPOOK |
| plurals with singulars: | RICK/STICKS |
| present with past tense: | RETURN/CONFIRMED |
| M with N: | DREAM/GLEAN |
| missed consonants: | PHRASE/DAZED |
| different spellings: | WEAR/WHERE |

Lyrics must be written with due respect for the rules of proper (not estuary) English. A whole evening based on rhymes that relied on poor pronunciation would be very tedious. Under no circumstances should the order of words in a phrase be inverted to contrive a rhyme, as in: 'it matters not' or 'it's the truth I'll learn'. Don't make life any more difficult for yourself than it need be. Remember that 'love' only rhymes with 'above', 'dove', 'glove', 'of' and 'shove'. Rather than agonize over trying to make something out of such a limited selection, it is better to write a song that expresses the meaning rather than uses the word.

## Metre

Metre is the number and pattern of stressed and unstressed syllables and words in a line or phrase (the stress being the **natural emphasis** that falls on **some** of them but not **oth**ers). This will be the same for each repeated block – all the A's will be exact repeats of the same pattern. This will make the words easier to hear and holds the song together, while at the same time moving it along. The stressed syllables are the places for the key words of the lyric to fall. The natural stress within the word must be matched to the accent of the music. You must learn to hear these stresses before you can apply them to lyrics.

| | | |
|---|---|---|
| **BE**WARE | U – | unstressed **stressed** |
| **WA**RY | – U | **stressed** unstressed |

102

| WHERETO**FORE** | ∪ ∪ − | unstressed unstressed **stressed** |
|---|---|---|
| **UN**DERWEAR | − ∪ ∪ | **stressed** unstressed unstressed |
| UN**WAR**Y | ∪ − ∪ | unstressed **stressed** unstressed |
| **WEAR**ING **OUT** | − ∪ − | **stressed** unstressed **stressed** |
| **WHEREBY** | − − | **stressed stressed** |

Traditionally, a line in which the last syllable of a line is stressed (be**ware**) is described as masculine, and one in which it is unstressed (**wary**) is described as feminine. (This terminology tends to be ignored now, but I mention it because you may find references to it elsewhere.)

To confound those whose grasp of metric and imperial measures is not entirely complete, metres also come in feet. The number of stresses in a line is described as the number of feet. Shakespeare wrote in iambic pentameters because there were five stresses or feet in each line.

The function of the musical setting is to complement the natural rhythm of the text. When lyrics are set, it is vital to match the stressed syllables to the strong beats of the music. For example:

**BAA** BAA **BLACK** SHEEP
**HAVE** YOU ANY **WOOL**?

rather than as in *Song and Dance*:

TELL ME **ON** A **SUNDAY PLEASE**

The sure sign of the inexperienced or careless lyricist is that words are hacked about to fit the metre, and contractions or fillers are used. You should not shorten words just because there are too many syllables, such as contracting 'over' to 'o'er'. (If you have to do this, you don't have too many syllables, you have the wrong word! Find another.) Similarly, if you have too few words you cannot give the lyric a light dusting of fillers like 'well', 'just' and 'hey' to sop up the beats. You cannot stre-e-e-e-etch wo-o-o-o-ords either.

It is hard to believe it, but WISHING YOU WERE SOMEHOW HERE AGAIN, in *The Phantom of the Opera* encapsulates in one line almost everything that you should not do. The word 'somehow' is a filler; it means nothing. Not only that, but the natural stress of the word falls on the first syllable whereas it is the second syllable that is accentuated by being given the highest note of the tune (a note which is also held). On top of all that, this line is the title of the number. You have to be an established name to get away with all that; don't you try it!

## Phonetics

(A repeat viewing of *My Fair Lady* is recommended before attempting this section.) Phonetics is the study of vocal sound and (as applied to lyrics) refers to the different contributions made by vowels and consonants. In singing vowels are used to produce the basic sounds, and the consonants chop it up into recognizable packages. In this process singers use their lips, teeth and tongue in varying combinations. When writing for singers, you should try not to make unrealistic demands upon them.

Some vowel sounds, like 'ah', are open; others, like 'ee', are closed. Since the open sounds are easier to produce, it is in your interest to ensure that they are used for sustained and high notes. In general the longer sounds are open and the shorter sounds are closed:

| *Open Sounds:* | | *Middle Sounds:* | |
|---|---|---|---|
| ah | AJAR, FAR | a | SAT, RARE |
| oh | ROW, OWN | eh | MEN, DEATH |
| oo | SHOE, CLUE | ir | BIRD, STIRRED |
| | | oy | COY, ANNOY |
| | | uu | PURR, HULL |

| *Closed Sounds:* | |
|---|---|
| ay | LAY, WAIT |
| ee | FEE, BEAN |
| iy | IF, BY |

Don't write lines or phrases in which all the consonants

huddle together. If you do, the words will run into each other, like MELT TOGETHER, and the audience will not understand them. Beware of ending one word with the same sound that the next one starts with, as in ENOUGH FOR, and of incompatible juxtapositions such as SMALL FEE. Make sure you aren't inadvertently creating different meanings, like 'be true to' ('beetroot'). (This is so common in pop songs that there is now a weekly newspaper column devoted to mis-hearings of lyrics; the old favourite POETRY IN MOTION perceived as OH! A TREE IN MOTION still tops the bill.)

Many singers have a problem with particular sounds like 'sts', 'ch', 'th' and even the seemingly simple 'p' or 's'. In *The Phantom of the Opera* there was a fear that Christine's lyric THOSE PLEADING EYES would be heard as THOSE BLEEDING EYES. Alan Jay Lerner said that when you finish a lyric, you should go back over it and take out as many words beginning with 's' as possible, because that is a sound that annoys the ear. It is in your interest that the lyric is communicated to the audience as clearly as possible. Give the singers as much help as you can.

## Working Methods

There are no hard and fast rules about how a song should be written. Do what works for you and your partner. It is a myth that all composers and lyricists create together round a piano. It can be a debilitating experience for two people to sit around waiting for inspiration to strike them both at the same time (you may need to practice with lightning first!) Generally one partner comes up with something in private (music or lyrics), and passes it on to the other one to work on, also in private. Then they meet to hear the results – and that's where the argument starts. The music is usually provided on cassette, and is only formally written down when the (first) final version is complete.

There is no obligation to start at the beginning of the show and work through to the end – indeed it is best to leave the opening number until you have completed a substantial part of the score. Start with whatever inspires you most and move on from there. Make it fun at the beginning; the hard slog will come soon enough.

The perfect lyric takes a great deal of crafting, and changes are made throughout the development and production process. You cannot expect your collaborators to sit around until your final work is available (Alan Jay Lerner took eight months to write ON A CLEAR DAY YOU CAN SEE FOREVER, discarding ninety-one complete lyrics). The tool you can use to solve this impasse is the dummy lyric. It has all the syllables, and demonstrates the rhyme scheme, so that it establishes the form of the lyric and the structure of the song, even though the content will change. Your composer can then go ahead and write the tune, while you await the inspiration. Oscar Hammerstein used to write a dummy lyric for Richard Rodgers to set, and only when he got the tune did he start work on the real lyric. The warning, though, must be that sometimes the dummy ends up in the show.

# 6 Making the Musical Work

Stephen Sondheim has said 'You spend two or three years working on a show until you think it's perfect, then you get into rehearsal and as soon as the actors start performing it you realize it's full of holes. So you have a frantic five weeks to fix it, and you finally get it right and you come to the first preview. Then as soon as there's an audience you realize it's full of holes again, and now you've got a week or ten days to fix it before the first night.'

## It's Never Finished

Consider the history of *Follies*. It was rewritten from the Broadway version before being presented in London. Major work was done in rehearsal, but by the first night it still didn't work properly, so, two months into the run, Sondheim and Goldman returned with more rewrites for another two weeks of rehearsal. After a year, during the cast change rehearsals, there were further rewrites. The worst part is that, in the end, it still didn't work – or recoup its production costs.

Similarly, *Sunset Boulevard* was revised for the Los Angeles production, and subsequently Broadway. At the first cast change in London, the show closed for three weeks for reworking, although in this instance the major alterations were to the physical production and staging.

The most radical changes in recent times were to *Martin Guerre*. Having received a critical drubbing, a new lyricist was brought in and the whole first act substantially rewritten, cutting away much dead wood, and focusing on the relationships of the three main characters. It was also restaged, minimizing the use of the previously constantly moving (and distracting) set. After five weeks of rehearsal while the show continued to play in the evenings, it closed for a week, and following a further week of 'previews', the new version – Mark II *Guerre*, as the creative team nicknamed it – had a second press night, four months after the first. Fortunately for all concerned the critics generally hailed it as a great improvement. This is a very high risk strategy though. When a second press night was held for *Ziegfeld*, after much rewriting, recasting and restaging – involving the efforts of two new directors – the critics thought it was worse than the original! Perhaps the ultimate example is *Candide*, which in its various productions has included contributions from the greatest talents of a whole generation of writers, yet is still not entirely satisfactory.

If Stephen Sondheim, Andrew Lloyd Webber, and Boublil and Schonberg have to do all that, you can see what a mountain you have to climb. But the lesson to be learned is the value of exposing the material to people who come to it totally fresh. That is what happens every night in performance. The audience is part of the creative process; as Moss Hart said, 'the vital scenes of a drama are played as much by the audience as by the actors on stage'. You are the person who has made the selection and assembly of material; you know the background, what's been put in, what's been left out; you know the complete history of the characters. Any time you read your work through, you subconsciously fill in the gaps. What you need is the reaction of someone who can't do that.

## The Reading

So how do you organize this exposure? The first stage is

the Reading. Assemble a group of people who don't know the material. Sit them down in your front room, and let them read it through aloud, while you just listen without taking part. Your readers will be reacting purely to what they see on the page, and your work will seem completely different to your expectations. You must try to assess it as an audience would, and see if what you were trying to say is coming across. You'll be in for a terrible shock, because it probably isn't.

The characters may seem totally different from what you had intended. You may find that what is supposed to be the leading role doesn't make the strongest impact; perhaps one of the other characters has ended up with the best lines or the best songs. You may find that the story is confused without the (unwritten) background. The dialogue which looks all right on the page may sound stilted and unnatural when spoken out loud. (Pam Gems has said that when she has written a new play she never knows if the dialogue will work until she's heard it read.)

A number of things will immediately become apparent to you as you watch, but question closely the people who are doing the reading. They may ask you 'What's happened to me? I haven't said a thing for pages!' or 'How come I'm saying that now when I was saying so and so then?' You should also quiz anyone who is watching. See how much they have received of the message that you were trying to convey; it may be dishearteningly little. And always tape the reading, so that you can listen to it again afterwards and really study what comes across and what doesn't.

Any professionals you can muster will be able to tell you more than civilians. I went to a reading of one of the many drafts of *Leonardo*. The millionaire behind the project wept openly with the emotion of the moment as the reading progressed, and afterwards his office staff likewise pronounced it a masterpiece. The professionals' opinions were all variations of 'You've got real problems here. You must decide what this is about.' Who did the millionaire believe? Don't do what he did; if you can, listen to the professionals.

## The Rewrites

Analyse what is missing. Go back to the storyline and the scene breakdown and see what you need to change. It is as important to plan your changes as it was to do the original planning. And there is nothing shameful about rewrites. It is a brave or foolish person who can't find a better, shorter or funnier way of conveying the existing information; or a better, shorter or funnier way of conveying more information.

You can quite often radically transform something with relatively small alterations. A brief exchange between two characters, referring to an incident in the past, can sketch in the whole background to a current dilemma or action. A line swapped from one person to another can change its meaning or dramatic effect. I know of an instance where the second half of one of the hero's speeches was given to the heroine. Instead of him appearing to lecture her, the fact that she understood and took up his idea immediately established that they were on the same wavelength, and developed the relationship between them. All that was achieved without a word being altered.

This is particularly true in establishing the authority of your leading characters. You may have unwittingly given subsidiary characters the best punch-lines or the plot points. Take them back! Keep the principal characters keyed into the action as much as possible – the leading characters must *lead*. You can't rely on the charisma of the performers to make that happen, it must be in the words.

As a result of the reading you may find that, despite your planning, a character's most important scene is happening off stage. It is always better for an audience to see something happening than to hear about it. If the conversion on the road to Damascus is in the story, it should be on the stage. For example, there are three key moments missing from *Miss Saigon*. Firstly, the driving force of the story is the relationship between Chris and Kim, which cannot simply be sexual – yet we see nothing to establish or support this. They meet, the lights go out, they go through a wedding ceremony. Secondly, we subsequently see Chris married to Ellen, but her character is not introduced, nor is their relationship hinted at beforehand. Thirdly, when Chris finds out that he has a child in Vietnam, he meets Ellen and walks off up stage to tell her in the wings. What a scene that should have been! These are vital elements of the story that the audience has not shared.

As you learn more about the characters and their story, you will find different and more effective ways of presenting them. Some things may have to be spelt out in more elaborate detail, while others are conveyed by a suggestion, and don't need the laboured explanation you have given. So it may be that scenes have to go, and songs have to go (and it's always your favourite that has to be cut) – but you must be tough on yourself. Sixty songs were written for *South Pacific*, and only fifteen of them were in the finished show.

You should set yourself clear objectives for what needs fixing in your next draft.

When you are reviewing or rewriting a scene ask yourself:

How does this further the action?

Is there a proper shape – a beginning, middle and end, building up to a climax that in turn leads on to the next scene?

What are each character's objectives and attitudes?

Does it serve more than one function, so as to keep the audience involved: exposition, character background, development, motivation, humour or conflict?

Is it clever, original, provocative and interesting?

You can easily become disheartened at this stage and lose enthusiasm. It is one of the stress points that the relationship with your writing partners must survive. You must be able to cope. You must have respect for each other's work and understand each other's needs. When the lyricist sends his meticulously honed lines to the composer, he must be ready for them to be returned with some words cut, because they 'didn't fit the tune', or with extra ones added. Keep the momentum of your writing partnership by setting deadlines. To give you all a goal to work to, fix a date for the next reading of the reworked material. Use different readers if possible, and see if your changes have had the desired effect.

Throughout the development process you will generate many different versions of your work; almost the most important single piece of advice is *never throw anything away*; rewrites can be rewritten (a new version), prewritten (an earlier rewrite) or dewritten (back to the original). More so than a play, a musical is a collage. Each piece that you change, in its turn changes how you see everything else. A version of a scene or song that doesn't work now, may at a later stage turn out to be what you need. You are on a journey for which you are drawing the map as you go along, and you may well at some time cut the bit that works and leave the bit that doesn't. It's a mistake that everyone has made. Later on, realizing you still have a problem, you may change that bit, and then what was originally cut is perfect.

While you are working on this stage of a show you may have to face what seems to be the ultimate horror: you hear that someone else is working on the same idea. What should you do? Unless your competitor is a major name (which would guarantee production of his or her version), you should carry straight on. No two people (or groups of collaborators) starting from the same source material will ever develop a project in the same way. You are unlikely to be subject to charges of plagiarism, and you have an equal chance of success. It is just as likely as not that, for some reason, the rival version may never come to anything. The collaborators may never realize their original concept and it may never be performed, or, even if it is produced, it may not work. Have faith in your abilities and use the competition as a spur to redouble your efforts.

## The director

Directors are the catalyst in the creative reaction. If

possible, try to get one involved in your project at an early stage. Nowadays most good directors have a creative input in the shaping of the material, not just an interpretative one – indeed they often demand it. Michael Blakemore is credited with the ideas of contrasting black and white with colour scenes, and of 'rewinding' the action in *City of Angels*. The rather overblown nature of *Aspects of Love* was Trevor Nunn's influence (Andrew Lloyd Webber has said that he thought of it as a chamber piece until Nunn became involved). Undoubtedly the reshaping of *Kiss of the Spider Woman* owed much to Hal Prince's influence, and Mike Ockrent is credited with 'co-conceiving' the new book of *Crazy for You* (it certainly has all his trademarks).

British and American directors have tended to come from different backgrounds. The great American directors have mostly worked previously in dance, for instance Jerome Robbins, Bob Fosse and Tommy Tune; Hal Prince is the exception. British directors in recent years have crossed over from straight dramatic theatre, often as a result of staging particular shows. For Trevor Nunn it was a small jump from the carriage in *Nicholas Nickleby* to the train in *Cats*. Michael Blakemore's expertise in handling the backstage farce *Noises Off* led to the behind-the-camera world of *City of Angels*. However, not all directors make the transition from plays to musical theatre as successfully as these.

## Private Workshops

The process of readings should go on until you are confident enough to move on to the next stage, which is a private workshop. For readings you can double up parts (as long as people aren't playing scenes with themselves), and a couple of people – the composer and lyricist if necessary – can sing the songs. A workshop should be on a bigger scale. There should be a minimum amount of doubling, and if possible you should use professional actors, under the guidance of a director, in some sort of space – a rehearsal room or church hall. With usually a week or two of rehearsal, to get the show on its feet, they will learn the music and give a rehearsed reading of the script. You will get more idea of the scale of the piece, as you will be able to hear the ensemble numbers as they should really sound.

Calling it a private workshop is deliberate, because with any workshop you need to define what it is you are trying to do: develop the material, or market it to investors, producers, and the theatre world in general. The purpose of a workshop is to see if the material works and to develop it. A workshop is not a performance, nor is it a showcase. It doesn't need to be held in a theatre and it certainly doesn't need sets, costumes, lighting, sound or an orchestra. All that is not only a complete waste of money, it actually confuses the issue. What you are doing in essence is simulating the beginning of the rehearsal process, up to the first run-through. So all you need is a group of performers, a piano and a space – two planks and a passion. It is useful to have some sort of audience, to give the actors someone to play to and (once again) to enable you to gauge how successfully your ideas are being communicated. However, this should be made up of friends and 'allied troops', not outsiders. Only when you have decided that the material works, should you go on and market it.

Too often people try to do both at the same time. They do one workshop and invite prospective producers or investors, as if the workshop were a showcase. If you haven't road-tested the material first, it may be only when it is in front of its target market of producers, agents, theatres, and so on that you find it still needs a lot of work. You can't at that point do six months more work on it and ask them all back again, because they won't come. Don't put anything on the market until it's ready. Like a car, you can only launch it once.

*Carmen Negra* was an example of what not to do. *Carmen Jones* added a new book and lyrics to Bizet's music, and set the result in a World War II factory against a boxing background; *Carmen Negra* was yet another variation, this time set in a football stadium in contemporary South America. It had twenty people in the cast, and twenty-two in the band, and it cost £35,000 to stage. The exercise killed the project off, rather than moving it forward, because what became clear was that the material wasn't ready to be seen in a performance situation. If it had been, a full-scale co-production with a repertory theatre could have been mounted for that sort of money.

In this country workshops and showcases are pretty free and easy affairs. Friends, or even strangers, are asked if they are interested in taking part, and, having considered the material, they say yes or no. Musical performers are generally very giving, and it is not unusual to have above-the-title West End names working for nothing in order to help the cause of new writing. It is all done on a handshake – they get travelling expenses, and hopefully a party afterwards, but no one expects anything further. In America it is far more regulated. There is an Equity contract that not only stipulates terms and conditions for the workshop or showcase but gives the performer first refusal of the part if the show goes into production (good for the actors, but not necessarily in the best interests of promoting new work).

If none of the writing team know any professionals personally, how do you make contact with someone to help you stage a workshop? You could try putting a notice on the stage-door notice-board of your local theatre, asking for volunteers. Alternatively, a small advertisement in *The Stage* newspaper could do the trick. You could also ask for a mention in *PCR*, the weekly casting information newsletter. Failing that, local amateur groups may have sufficient time and talent to take on an additional project. (Showcases, though, because they have more riding on them, must be of an appropriate standard, and are probably best left to an experienced professional to organize.)

## Making a Demo Tape

At this stage of the development process you should

consider the Demo Tape. Again, you do need this to be done by professionals, but it doesn't need Abbey Road studios, a cast of thousands and the London Symphony Orchestra. What you are doing is demonstrating the melody and lyrics for the benefit of potential producers, agents, investors and any other interested party who may be able to help you realize your dream. You need no more than four singers and a piano, in a small studio. Anything else is a waste of money.

Don't record all the numbers – just a representative selection of perhaps six songs, combining solos and duets. There should be a mixture of ballads (to demonstrate that you can write tunes); rhythm numbers to provide contrast; and comedy numbers (to show your wit). Nobody will want to hear the whole score when you first approach them. Make sure that you have fully rehearsed what you are going to do beforehand, unless you are using regular session singers (which at this stage is unlikely); you don't want to waste valuable studio time while the performers learn the material.

Use the demo, like the readings for market research. Try to elicit as critical a judgement as possible, asking people to rate the songs over a range of categories – melody, lyrics, originality and so on – on a scale of one to ten. You need something specific: 'very nice, quite catchy' will not be much help to you. See if everyone is telling you the same thing. Also find out if you have unwittingly plagiarised something (only writers with big reputations – and bank balances – who have access to top lawyers can do that and get away with it).

## Reader's Report

There is a story of a young American kid who had a great idea for a musical. He took the finished script to a friend who lived down the street and then went back next day for an unbiased professional opinion of his work. The neighbour looked him straight in the eye and said, 'It's the worst thing I've ever read', after which he proceeded to teach the kid more about musical theatre in one afternoon than most people learn in a lifetime. Unfortunately, not everyone has Oscar Hammerstein for a neighbour, nor does every kid grow up to be Stephen Sondheim.

So how can you find help? You could commission a reader's report. This is a professional written appraisal of your script and tape, considering concept, style, storyline, writing, construction, characterization, presentation and commercial potential, with recommendations for further development. It has two uses. Firstly it will offer a fresh professional response to your work so far, and hopefully provoke you to further ideas of how to improve it (this is another part of the process of exposing your material to a wider audience). Secondly (assuming it is favourable), it will be of use when you come to the next stage: marketing your project (see Chapter 7). You will be able to show that your work is able to stand up to professional scrutiny.

## During Production

Assuming you market the work successfully (which you will be able to do once you have read Chapter 7), a producer commits himself to putting on the show. This does not mean that project development comes to an end – far from it. The process moves up a gear as the producer assembles a creative team of director, choreographer, musical director and designers. As more people become involved, the pace quickens, opportunities (and dangers) multiply. The main creative drive will come from the director, but each of the team will have ideas about the contribution that their department can make to realizing the show. (At least they should do. I remember an exploratory meeting between the director and writers of one project and a well-known set designer whose first words were, 'I don't see how you're going to do this.' After a couple of hours' discussion in which we laid out our ideas, he went away to think it through further, but when we met again a week later, his first words were, 'I still don't see how you're going to do this'. We decided to look for another designer.) When the creative team's ideas do start flowing, you must be open-minded and welcome their visions of how the show can best be staged. As each element of the show is assembled, decisions will be taken which may necessitate further development and rewriting.

When you reach the rehearsal stage, you will realize why the word 'theatre' is shared with hospitals. Generally it is blood and guts everywhere, and the instruments seem to do more harm than good. In spite of having a clear idea of what you are going to do, it is never quite the same once you are inside, and there are always complications. Transplants and amputations are common, and dramatic attempts at resuscitation are often called for. Ultimately, you feel that 'Casualty' or 'Accident and Emergency' would be more appropriate terms than 'theatre'.

It is at this point that a doctor may be called for. If serious problems emerge during rehearsal or pre-London performances, and the producer feels that the creative team does not seem to be able to conquer them, he may decide to bring in help. Enter the book (or script) doctor. This is usually someone whom the producer or director has worked with before and whose opinion they respect. Unencumbered by all the past history, they will look at the show as it stands and make suggestions for fixing it.

The arrangement can be formal or informal. At its simplest, someone may watch both performances on a matinee day, and chat about areas of concern over dinner afterwards. This may be followed up with a few written suggestions. No fee is involved; it is just someone helping out a friend. The other extreme is a formal contract to rewrite the book, and this may involve a co-writing credit, in which case the new writer will split the royalty with the original one. The most drastic option is to replace the original writer. This is usually resolved financially by a one-off buy-out payment or an ongoing royalty; James Fenton (who wrote the original lyrics for *Les Miserables* and was replaced by Herbert Kretzmer) wisely opted for the latter, and is now believed to be a millionaire as a result. Although I doubt if this made Herbert Kretzmer any more sanguine when he was replaced as the lyricist of *Martin Guerre*.

## *Questionnaires*

Once your work is being performed before a real paying audience, it is a good idea to poll its members night by night. Obviously you do not ask every single person in the audience to fill in a form, because it would require too many people to process the results, but twenty questionnaires given out with programmes in different parts of the house should produce enough responses to be useful.

Figure 9 is an example of a preview questionnaire. You will notice that it attempts to separate the respondents' reactions to material and interpretation – an important distinction to make. A simplified version, leaving out the interpretative element, can be used for showcases and workshops. It is not wise to follow the film industry, and rewrite the whole thing on the strength of one comment, but if twenty people say the same thing you should take it seriously – especially if they have misunderstood your intentions. It is also useful to know if opinions change in the second act, because most people fill in the questionnaires during the interval. Regular polling will enable you to track the changes you make during pre-London seasons and previews. In all the heady excitement, it is useful to see if rewrites actually do have the desired effect on how the audience perceives what you are doing.

## Post-production

Assuming the show is successful, and interest is shown in an overseas production, the creative team usually takes a long hard look at the show to see if there are any changes that could or should be made to improve the show. Often lack of time has prevented all your ideas being introduced, or there may be ideas considered and discarded during the production process that, in retrospect, should have been implemented. Alternatively, there may be a need to enhance the product for a different audience.

The prospective American co-producers of *Me and My Girl* were concerned that they would be paying for a cast

119

## Figure 9    Audience Questionnaire

The Creative Team would value your response to the production.
Please indicate below how you would rate the following:

| | **Poor** | **Fair** | **Good** | | **Poor** | **Fair** | **Good** |
|---|---|---|---|---|---|---|---|
| Music | | | | Direction | | | |
| Lyrics | | | | Choreography | | | |
| Dialogue | | | | Cast | | | |
| Story | | | | Settings | | | |
| Construction | | | | Costumes | | | |
| Characters | | | | Lighting | | | |
| Entertainment | | | | Sound | | | |

Will you recommend this show to your friends?

What was the best feature of the show?

What was the worst feature of the show?

Did you feel that Act II was better than Act I, or not so good?

Have you any further comments?

Thank you for your participation. Please hand this form to a member
of the front-of-house staff as you leave.

of thirty-eight, but the chorus didn't appear for about forty minutes in the middle of Act I. They asked for a new chorus number to be inserted somewhere in that gap. The writers found a solution, and the number 'Hold My Hand' was inserted for the Australian production; a revised version of the 'Lamp Post Ballet' in Act II (already changed once between the original Leicester production and London) was also introduced. Both were deemed successful, the Americans approved, and the show opened in New York. These alterations were then incorporated into the original production at the next cast change.

## Let someone else make the mistakes

While you are developing your work you should always be on the lookout for help and inspiration. As with any endeavour, it's vital to learn as much about the field as possible. Go and see as many shows as you can, and learn from other people's mistakes; it is astonishing how many people writing musicals never go and see any. If someone says that they hate musicals, or that they never go to the theatre, you know they are wasting their time. Even worse is the person who claims to know all there is to know about music; it is usually someone from the pop world looking towards the theatre for some sort of artistic credibility or respectability.

You can always benefit from finding out how someone else tackled a problem. There is more to be learnt from the bad shows, because it's usually easier to identify what went wrong (it's more difficult to pin down what went right in the good shows). The development of *Valentine's Day* is worth studying. In the pre-London version, at Chichester, it was a dull but competent adaptation of Shaw's play *You Never Can Tell*, with its central theme of the confrontation between Valentine and Gloria, a 'new woman'. However, the creative team obviously fell in love with the secondary character of the butler. They wrote in umpteen irrelevant numbers for him, gave him top billing, and Valentine (whose day it was supposed to have been) didn't get a look in. The result was a complete mess; a third of the audiences regularly left at the interval, and it ran for about three weeks.

You should also read about how other people have done it (consult the bibliography at the end of this book for some of the possible sources). Finding out how shows that you know and admire (or even dislike) came to be written and produced can help you to make the most of your ideas. Learning about other writers' working methods is a useful insight into how you can shape yours. You may also take some solace from how difficult things were for them.

# 7  Marketing

There is a story of a writer who, after slaving away for months, finally completes his play. Desperate for recognition, he calls his best friend and says, 'I've written a play'. The friend's response is: 'But why, when there are so many already?' You will soon find that not everyone is even as enthusiastic as that. If you thought writing was hard work, it's nothing compared to getting your work produced. This is where the perspiration turns into a muck sweat. Of every five shows produced in the West End, three lose money, one breaks even, and one makes a profit; producers are therefore understandably wary.

## The Public Showcase

How do you get people interested in your work? You can try staging a public showcase. Essentially a showcase is a rather more grown-up version of a workshop. It gives you an opportunity to offer prospective buyers a taste of the fruits of your labours. But when you stage a showcase you must think very carefully about what you choose to include and how you choose to present it – above all, you must be sure that your material is ready to be exposed to the view of a particularly knowledgeable and critical sort of public. When you go fishing for a producer, you need to bait the hook very carefully.

You want professional actors, musical director and director, and you need to have a full cast of characters (although choruses of twenty should be avoided). Like a workshop, a showcase should be done on an informal basis, with just a piano. There should be no production values – no sets, no costumes, no choreography – because, once it becomes a performance, people will judge it in performance terms, instead of in terms of the material. Production values only confuse the issue. (Anyway, with the time and resources at your disposal, you cannot successfully compete with a full-scale production, so don't try.) In a strange way, having the actors keep the scripts in their hands (even if they don't actually need to refer to them) helps to take the performance curse off the thing. In any case, the audience you are dealing with will be made up of professionals. They should be able to make the imaginative leap from what you are presenting to a performance; if they can't, they won't be any use to you.

Anyone trying to cover up deficiencies is not ready for a showcase. If you can't sell the idea of *Miss Saigon* without the helicopter, it isn't a very good idea. Go back to your concept. Sell them the idea, and illustrate how you developed it. (One of the fundamental problems of the Vivian Ellis Workshop is the staging; the judges so often comment on the staging, when what they are supposed to be considering is the writing.)

I went to the showcase of a musical which had reincarnation as its theme. The hero and heroine had met before in Germany in the thirties, where naturally he was a Nazi and she was a Jew. There was a song which was actually staged with dancing stormtroopers. Afterwards, the only thing anyone remembered was the 'Springtime For Hitler' number. Their attention had been hijacked. No one engaged with the ideas of the story or the quality of the writing, the staging had obscured rather than displayed the material.

The reason for doing a showcase is that you can reach a lot of people in one go, and hopefully create some hype. This is the theatre, and a live rendition of the material will be more effective than reading a script and listening to a demo. (At a later stage, doing a similar sort of live demo for prospective investors can be an equally effective way of raising money.) Never underestimate the effectiveness of getting a group of people in a room and singing at them; word of mouth is the most effective selling tool there is – whether for washing powder or theatre tickets. You can advertise all you like with no effect, but if someone's best friend says that your product gives the whitest wash or best night out they've ever had, you make a sale. It's also important to remember that, even if you don't sell this particular show, you may interest someone in your talent. Charles Hart did not win the Vivian Ellis prize, but his work so impressed Andrew Lloyd Webber (who was one of the judges) that he asked him to co-write the lyrics for *The Phantom of the Opera*. Not bad for a second prize!

It is often easier to persuade someone to attend a showcase, which happens at a fixed time, than to get around to reading a script. However, people can usually come up with a convincing excuse for not being able to come at one particular time, so try doing more than one showcase, and at different times of day. Lunchtime and at the end of the working day or in the early evening period are good choices.

It is a mistake to perform the whole show. It only reinforces the performance aspect. (Also, people are more likely to allow you forty-five minutes of their time than two-and-a-half hours without an interval they could use for escape.) You should consider carefully what you present, and this will depend on your material. Sometimes it is best to do an abridged Act I, and then say 'If you want to find out what happens in the end you'll have to option the show.' *Spin of the Wheel* (a story about a game-show contestant) did this so successfuly that it *was* optioned. Unfortunately, though, Act 2 hadn't been written, and the writers were never able to bring the story to a suitable conclusion, or match the quality of their original writing. When it was produced, the show flopped.

Sometimes it's better to present a condensed version of the whole story, introduced by a narrator. You must make sure that you use a confident presenter and have a well-crafted, clear narration. It must capture the spirit of your work fully and explain the story effectively.

Whichever method you choose, the presentation should be music-heavy, since it is the songs that will sell the show.

When compiling the guest list, you need to aim for a mix of all the different people who might help you to move the project ahead – producers, theatres, publicists, publishers and money. Ideally, at the end of the show you want Cameron Mackintosh rushing up to you saying, 'You must let me produce this', as Jude Kelly asks, 'Any chance of starting at West Yorkshire Playhouse?', Baz Bamigboye promises, 'You'll be heading my column on Friday', Richard Toeman declaims, 'I'll top any offer from Warner Chappell', and a little old lady bringing up the rear takes a bundle of notes from her handbag and asks, 'Is this enough to become an investor?' That's the kind of hope that keeps us all going – so dream on.

To come anywhere near that scenario, however, you must explore every avenue to identify the people you should ask to the showcase. Check advertisements, programmes and *The Stage* to find the names of useful people committed to new writing in the musical theatre, and lean on anyone you know who can give you a personal entree (the cast may have some useful friends). Then get hold of a copy of *Contacts* (published by *The Spotlight*). As its title implies, this lists the names and addresses of producers, theatres, agents and so on. Sit down and work your way through it.

Always use invitations, so that you know who was invited, and who came. Then you can do a follow-up afterwards. Make sure the information you send out is entirely clear as to what the show is about (the concept again), who the writers are, how many people there are in the cast, and how long the showcase will last. Don't be afraid to use hard-sell tactics. You will also find it useful to develop some selling copy. This is a few sentences (a paragraph at most) of the kind you find on handbills, or throwaways. It should amplify your concept, intrigue the reader and tempt him to come and find out what it is all about.

If you can come up with a striking way of delivering the

invitation, allied to the theme of your show, and include an entertaining letter incorporating your selling copy, this should hopefully attract enough attention to ensure attendance. Any direct-mail letter must be one page only. It should start with the strongest point as a hook, in contrast to a speech which finishes with the strongest point as a summation. If you do not receive a response, fire off a fax a few days before the event, and follow that up with a phone call. You must become thick skinned if you want to sell your material.

Where you stage the showcase is just as important as what you do and how you do it. The less-than-successful *Carmen Negra* workshop, mentioned previously, was staged in a thousand-seater theatre. Obviously there weren't a thousand 'useful' people who could be invited, so it was filled up with a supposedly sympathetic audience of actors and chums. However, the material wasn't ready to be seen, so the audience became unsettled, and then the performers started sending up the material; finally the audience became totally out of control, with laughing, whistling and cat-calling. It was an awful feeling to be part of it, and to see the show go down the drain.

Tommy Tune has said that he considers the venue for a workshop or showcase is vital to its success. Because of the performance expectation, he never uses theatres and prefers to find a sympathetic environment. For *Grand Hotel* he did both workshop and showcase in a disused hotel ballroom of the period. This was so successful that he went on to develop a set and staging concept similar to that ballroom, which is where the pillars and the chairs came from.

At the showcase, before you start, you must recap once again for your audience what you are presenting and how you are presenting it (they will undoubtedly have lost or forgotten the material you sent them). Do provide a programme, so that they have something to take away; it should contain the concept and selling copy, your contact details, and biographies of both the creative team, and (in return for giving their services) the cast. Also, make sure you do not miss this opportunity to develop your project. Make your guests work for their free show. Always use a questionnaire, so that you can gauge feedback. Refreshments afterwards can be used to encourage your audience not to rush away, and this often results in some useful contacts and responses.

## Be your own producer

But what if, on the day, all this doesn't work? Either producers don't come, or those who do, say it was a great evening, and do invite them next time, but they don't offer you a production. Unfortunately, both of these are frequent occurrences. Where do you go from there?

You need to look very carefully at your audience response. You may need to do further development work before you try again. Alternatively, if the response is good but doesn't succeed in moving the project into production, you could try doing it yourself. Don't fall off your chair! A small-scale fringe production (a rather more grown-up version of a showcase) could be the next step. With luck it could be reviewed, attract public attention and perhaps be picked up by a producer and moved on to a wider market. This has been done successfully on a number of occasions, but even this golden scenario is still only an opportunity. No long-term riches are guaranteed. Consider the progress of *Burning Blue*.

*Burning Blue* was a play about homosexuality in the American Navy. It opened to notices of the best play of the year at the King's Head Theatre, and all seemed set for a smooth transition to the West End. Unfortunately, the producer who took it up chose the Theatre Royal, Haymarket, for a home. This was far too big a venue for the limited-interest market – with 850 seats (more per performance than the King's Head had in a week) and completely the wrong ambience. The result was more rave reviews, film rights sold, and closing notices posted after about eight weeks. Attempts to resuscitate the show by moving to the 450-seater Ambassadors Theatre (the sort of venue it should have gone to in the first place) also failed because the impact had by then been dissipated.

Fringe productions are both easier and more difficult than you might think. Fringe theatre exists almost entirely on the desire of its participants – be they actors, directors or writers – to have their work seen. It is not a financially viable proposition. The good news is that it is less difficult than you might imagine to assemble a group of people to put on a show. Even so, there is the risk that, after you have succeeded in finding good people to commit themselves to maybe two weeks' of rehearsal and a three-week run for next to nothing, they may get an offer of well-paid work and drop out. Also, demand for venues is stronger than you might imagine. In spite of rentals that are often quite high (given the rather poor facilities on offer), they are frequently booked up for some months ahead.

You therefore have to consider carefully both the financial commitment and the effort involved before deciding to go ahead; if you don't have the knowledge or contacts to do it yourself, you should hire someone to manage it for you. As with a showcase, there is no point in taking it on if the production is not of a high enough standard, and the marketing is not good enough to secure you an audience. Nonetheless, with sufficient help, extraordinarily hard work and some good luck mounting a fringe production can be very rewarding. A word of caution, though. Budget on funding the entire cost yourself, and look on any box-office receipts as a bonus.

Figure 10 is an outline budget for a fringe production. It is based on a cast of eight and a pianist/musical director (working on expenses only) for a two-week rehearsal period and a three-week run, with everything begged, borrowed or stolen, and you producing. (Don't underestimate the amount of help you will need; be prepared to call in favours!) The total cost may seem a lot, but (given what some people spend on demos and one-off showcase performances) you are at least getting something reasonably substantial for your money.

## Figure 10   Fringe Production Budget

**REHEARSAL COSTS**
Expenses; cast; stage management;
copying; petty cash. **600**
**CREATIVE TEAM EXPENSES**
Director; choreographer; MD;
costume/set designers. **250**
**PHYSICAL PRODUCTION COSTS**
Set construction; costumes; props;
lighting; fit-up; transport. **800**
**ADVERTISING AND PROMOTION**
Marketing; publicity; advertising;
printing; distribution; programmes **650**
**THEATRE COSTS**
Rent/staff wages/box office **3,000**
**PLAYING COSTS**
Expenses; cast; S/Ms; wardrobe; MD,
consumables. **990**
**CONTINGENCY**
5% **315**

**TOTAL PRODUCTION COSTS** **6,605**


**ESTIMATED FUNDING**

**THEATRE INCOME**
Box Office (50% @ £6.00); programmes. **5,850**
**SPONSORSHIP**
Commercial Companies; other sources **750**

**TOTAL FUNDING** **6,600**

Your inspiration should be *A Slice of Saturday Night*. The writers funded a production in their local fringe theatre in Brighton. (Of course it's easy to find a cast there: you need an Equity card before you can buy a house in Brighton.) It was well enough received for them to decide to hire a London fringe venue for a four-week season. That was well reviewed, and the show moved to the West End. It has since been produced all over the world. It's a shame that it wasn't a very good show.

If you have sufficient stamina and a big enough budget, you could think about a production on the biggest fringe of all – Edinburgh. This would cost you a good deal more, because – in addition to the above budget – you will have to transport, accommodate, feed and water the cast and crew. It will also mean considerably more work. It does, however, offer you a bigger opportunity to be seen and taken up, especially if you win a fringe first. The disadvantage is that you face unbelievable competition for an audience from twelve hundred other shows; all the time you are not performing, you will need to be out on the streets promoting the show. It will be a tremendous experience, though, and you may make some useful contacts.

With the agreement of the cast and musicians, you should always record (and if possible video) the performance for future reference. The results can help you to refine the show, because exposing it to an audience is bound to inspire you to change it. They will also provide back-up ammunition, if someone shows an interest in the material. You must realize, though, that this can never be used to launch a first strike on a potential producer, since live performance recordings without the benefit of retakes will inevitably contain imperfections. All the same, since you have singers who can really get the most out of the material, it's a good opportunity to go into a studio to make a new demo.

## Producers and how to approach them

When you come to approach producers direct, you need to consider some background information on your market-place. In the current economic climate – with the spectres of the great flops of all time like *Bernadette, Children of Eden* and *Out of the Blue* still hovering – no one is actively looking for anything. Even so, producers are still inundated with new material. The Really Useful Group receives about half-a-dozen scripts a week, in spite of the fact that they have never yet produced a single musical that was not written by Andrew Lloyd Webber. Cameron Mackintosh Ltd do not even open submissions, for fear of being sued for stealing ideas.

Theatre production is a cottage industry. Banish any ideas, derived from MGM backstage musicals, of palatial office suites above theatres, in which impresarios entertain chorus girls (or more likely chorus boys) on *chaises longues*. There is not a single West End producer who employs someone full-time specifically to read scripts. Even the biggest producers only employ between six and twelve people in their office, and they have to do everything. Set the number of people against the mountain of material, and you can see the problem.

What usually happens is that producers keep submissions for ages before they get around to considering them. Eventually someone looks at the first half-a-dozen pages of the script, and perhaps listens to the first two songs on the demo, before sending it back with a non-committal note saying that 'it doesn't fit in with our current production plans'. This is no good to the authors, and no real good to the producers either. The conundrum is that, although no one is looking for anything, everyone will want a winning show, if they can be made aware of its existence. How do you solve it?

Psychology plays a part. Looking at new material is usually homework for the weekend. So you approach a producer with a package that makes the homework easier and more interesting. This is where the concept comes in again. You try to arouse interest in the idea, which will only at a later stage lead on to the script.

You put together a Treatment, which is a synthesis of all the things discussed so far. It should be long enough to give a real flavour of your idea, but short enough to whet their appetite. It should contain:

*The Concept*: e.g. a musical version of the *Satanic Verses*, with a cast of ten, employing Middle-Eastern music, in a through-written form.

*The Storyline*, including the titles of the numbers (as on a show-album sleeve) and perhaps a few snatches of witty dialogue.

*The List of Characters*, with a brief description based on the Character Background.

*The Demo Tape*, with no more than six songs, choosing the strongest and most varied.

The whole package should be no longer than five pages – if it is more easily digested, it is more likely to be looked at. The accompanying letter (again using your selling copy) should be of one page. If the idea is of interest, then the producer will ask for the script and perhaps a longer demo. (I was pleased to see that Richard Stilgoe's advice to entrants in the Quest For New Musicals was virtually identical to what I've been saying for years.)

Do make sure that whatever you're sending is well presented, as detailed in Chapter 9. It should also be in English. (I received a musical version of *The Hunchback of Notre Dame* in Spanish, which I am not euro-friendly enough to understand.)

## Agents

So far, I have been talking about approaching producers direct. But you have more chance of a producer treating your material seriously if it comes via an agent. This shows that it has already successfully survived one screening process, and a particular producer may respect a particular agent's judgement. More material is produced as a result of personal recommendation than for any other reason (if you look in the programme when you have just seen something unstageable, you will usually find that the producer/director/writer/agent have worked together before). If you can get an agent, therefore, the commission will be well spent. If you know anyone who has an agent, ask them for suggestions about whom to approach, and whether they will give you an introduction. Before doing so they will no doubt want to look at a treatment, and possibly a reader's report before they commit themselves.

## Foot in the door

Whichever route you take – producer or agent – never send anything to anyone without ringing them first. This saves the time, effort and money you can waste by approaching the wrong people. Don't fall into the actor's casting trap. There persists in the minds of some actors a belief that if they can just get into an audition, their talent will be recognized, and they will be offered the part. It doesn't matter that the part demands a five-foot-two blond singer; if the six-foot-four dark, tone-deaf actor can just get in front of the director, he will suddenly see it differently and give him the job. It doesn't work for actors, and it won't work for you. Don't bombard everyone on earth with your show, and expect that, once they've read it, they'll want it.

Turn to *Contacts* and the *Writers' and Artists' Yearbook* and go through their listings of literary agents. Ring up some of those who are listed and see if they are prepared to look at your material. Most only handle novelists and playwrights, and in any case may not want to take on anyone new, but there may be someone who is interested. It's worth checking the artists' agents listings as well, because a number of them handle directors and writers too.

Whenever you ring anyone, always have your concept and selling copy to hand. Be prepared to dazzle them with a few well-rounded sentences, and expect them to ask questions. A ready answer can make all the difference, as can catching them off guard. Try calling after 6.30 p.m., when the slaves have usually gone home and the boss may well answer his own telephone. Then pitch straight in; ask if he would like the treatment first, or the complete script. Always get the name of the person to send it to. Some companies are simply an umbrella organization, providing office support for a number of separate independent agents, and you must find the right one. The message here is targeting. If, after reading the treatment, an agent wants to read a script, make the most of the opportunity. Take it round personally and introduce yourself.

Use the same approach with producers. Find out who is interested in musicals, because many won't touch them. Repertory theatres generally have only one or two musical slots a year. It's very unlikely that they could afford to take the chance on a new musical, unless it was a co-production with a West End management. However, an encouraging development is that some are beginning to mount low-budget, fringe-style productions in their studios.

Never send out your only copy of anything. Expect things to be 'lost in the post', or, more likely, lost after they have reached their destination. You should send a stamped, addressed envelope for the return of your material – although that doesn't necessarily mean it *will* be sent back. Frankly, given that scripts will be worn out after about three trips, and that postage is so expensive, you could just take pot luck. Give the agent or producer a call after a month if you have heard nothing, and monthly thereafter. Keep prodding gently – after all, it's no good letting your impatience get the better of you and demanding it back.

Approaching a publisher direct is not usually very productive, unless your name is already known. Publishers are generally only interested in material that has already been successfully performed and has thus proved itself to have a ready market in either the professional or amateur fields. The same is true of record companies. They are only interested in material that has immediate selling potential, and there will be no one who has any knowledge or interest in the theatre. On the odd occasions when a record company has taken a financial interest in a show (usually written by someone with pop credibility but no theatre experience), it has been a complete disaster. Record companies are now reluctant to produce even cast albums of successful shows, since in their terms the market is too small. That is why specialist labels such as First Night and Dress Circle have taken over this role.

## Bankability – how to increase interest

One way of generating more interest in your project, is to make it more attractive by trying to build some bankability into it. You could try to find a name artist for a leading role, or a well-known director who might come on board. They can be contacted through their agent via *Spotlight*. Names are usually booked up a year ahead and are always being besieged with projects; on the other hand, they usually have the financial independence to work on what interests them, and if you spark their imagination they may take it up.

The record for the length of time taken to get from first idea to first night is believed to be held by Meredith Wilson for *The Music Man* – seven years. It took Mark Bramble six years with *Barnum*. He had to build it brick by brick; initially he couldn't find any collaborators – Cy Coleman, Charles Strouse, Harvey Schmidt, Burton Lane and Michael Stewart all turned him down – but he finally managed to sell it to producer David Merrick just as an idea, on the strength of his draft book. Merrick suggested Jim Dale for the lead, and Bramble spoke to Jim Dale, who joined on the strength of Merrick's name. Bramble then went back to Cy Coleman and Michael Stewart, who came on board on the strength of their names, and the actual writing began.

What if your address book doesn't have those kind of phone numbers in it? You may have to rely on the scientific miracle of pure blind chance. Michael Sloan was an actor friend of mine who, some years ago, wanted to get into film production. He had co-written a short and was trying to raise some money to shoot it; meanwhile he was working in the basement of Selfridges department store. Who should come in one day but Edward Woodward. Naturally Michael had a script with him, which he pressed on to the wary Woodward to read. The next day Woodward rang Michael, saying that he would like to play the lead. On the strength of his name the money was raised and the film made. It would make a nice end to the story if Michael was now a Hollywood producer. Well, dear reader, he is – and if you see a re-run of *The Equalizer*, starring Edward Woodward, you'll see Michael's name as creator/producer. As someone once said, 'Luck is when preparation meets opportunity'. And remember that, when a commentator remarked on Jack Nicklaus' luck, he replied, 'It's funny – the more I practice, the luckier I become'.

Don't be afraid of the blunderbuss principle. Try all avenues at once. If you stick to approaching one person at a time, someone else will be reading your will, before you are reading an offer. Instead of worrying about five different people showing interest at the same time, wait until it happens and then worry. Meanwhile, use anything to further the cause: build up contacts, attend courses, join writers' groups, follow the trade journals, get involved in musical theatre in any way you can. As Mike Hewett said: 'The writing was the easy part. What got it produced was a lot of bloody-minded, relentless, damn-you-all persistence. That, far more than mere writing ability, is probably the most essential requirement for any would-be writer.' Nothing is ever wasted. Tomorrow could be the day you meet the person who makes it all happen.

# 8 Contracts, Casting, Rehearsals, Previews and the First Night

When asked 'What comes first – the music or the lyrics?', Sammy Cahn always replied: 'First comes the contract.' If you're reading this book, you're probably not at the stage of being commissioned to write something. But, although rights, options, royalties and so on aren't actually part of the creative process, you can't get something performed – which is, after all, what you are aiming at – without them being involved. Then almost inevitably, it becomes like something out of a Marx Brothers film: the contract scene in *A Night At the Opera*, – 'the party of the first part ... the party of the second part ... say whose party is this?', and 'Don't worry about that; it's just the sanity clause – Hey, Boss, everybody knows there ain't no Santa Claus.'

## The contract

Anything that involves lawyers raises this spectre of Otis P. Driftwood or Rufus T. Firefly. The first time I was involved in drawing up a writer's contract, I wanted it to be as simple and user-friendly as possible. When I sent it to the lawyer, it was six pages long, but when it came back it was twenty-seven pages long. If that isn't creative writing I don't know what is! The subject of contracts is too complex to go into minute detail here, but, as this is the next step on your journey to the first night, here is a brief outline of the basic principles.

When you first have your idea, and before you start work on it, you should agree with your collaborators how you are going to share your credits and spoils. If there are three of you (book, music and lyrics) you don't want to reach the stage of selling the material and then find that two of you are expecting a one-third share of the proceeds each, while the other one is expecting a half! It's the same with billing; you don't want to find that you all expect to be billed first. Don't think it couldn't happen – it will, if you don't do something about it. Get all that out of the way before you start, and get it in writing. Likewise, if there are three agents involved, make it plain that you don't want them competing with each other. Come to a consensus agreement before you start, and have one agent do a deal in principle for all three.

Above all don't be too greedy. Bear in mind that getting anything produced nowadays is a miracle. You can't afford to act like Andrew Lloyd Webber until you *are* Andrew Lloyd Webber. There was the case of a repertory production of a new show, in which (astonishingly) interest was shown by both a West End and a New York producer. The writers were convinced that they had *Cats* and *The Phantom of the Opera* rolled into one, and they were so determined that they were not going to be taken for a ride that, after extraordinarily protracted negotiations, both producers eventually pulled out. The show has never been produced.

Whether you are dealing with West End, repertory or Fringe, there is some sort of writers' organization/producers' organization basic contract that outlines minimum terms and conditions. Generally it's the Writers' Guild and SOLT (The Society of London Theatre), TMA (The Theatre Managers' Association) or ITC (Independent Theatre Council). Unless you are a name and have clout, you won't be in any position to bargain anything above these basic terms. Bear in mind that the writer's payments referred to in these agreements – fees, royalties, and so on – will be split between book, music and lyric

139

writers. The producer's lawyer will put together a contract that covers every foreseeable (and many improbable) eventualities, in case the show goes on to become the world's greatest money-spinner. This does not guarantee that it will, of course.

The first main section is the option to produce the show. This usually lasts for two years, with a possible further extension if necessary. This is to give the producer time to juggle availabilities in order to assemble the creative team and cast that he wants. Hal Prince, Madonna and Pavarotti will all be booked up a long way ahead. The fee for the option will be probably around £2,000 each to book, music and lyric writers, payable on signing the contract. There will also be a similar figure payable on the first day of rehearsals, and on the West End opening night, but these will be non-returnable advances against future royalties. The option will cover a provincial try-out and a West End run. There is no guarantee of a production, or of the second and third payments. If it isn't produced within the specified period, the rights revert to you, and you can start trying to sell it all over again to someone else.

The second main section of the contract deals with royalty payments. This is a percentage of the weekly gross box-office takings (after deduction of VAT and ticket-agents' commission). That means all the money taken at the box office, for the eight performances of that particular week, less VAT, and whatever commission the ticket agents are entitled to. The Writers will probably receive around 7½%, split between them; the Director will probably get 2%, the Choreographer 1%, and the Designers ½% each. To give you some idea of the possible maximum figure involved, one of the most profitable shows in recent years was *Oliver!* at the London Palladium. At its peak it was taking £365,000 gross per week and selling out the biggest commercial theatre in London at all eight shows a week. That was exceptional.

There is usually a waiver built into all royalty agreements, whereby, if payment would result in the show going into loss, you agree to forgo it. What often happens, is that the show opens to mixed notices and poor business. The producer supports it in the hope of long-term success, and it may go on for weeks, but you never receive any royalties.

Profit is the gross box-office takings, less VAT, commissions, royalties and the weekly running costs (theatre rent, salaries, equipment hire, advertising and so on). Until the investors have been repaid, all weekly profits go to them. Thereafter (that is, once the show has recouped its investment) profits are split 60:40 between the producer and the investors. At this point there is usually a rise in creative royalties. This is where bargaining power comes into play, but the writers could probably expect a rise from 7½% to 10% or so – again, split between them. On a moderately expensive, reasonably successful show it may well take as long as nine months to recoup the investment.

The third main section of the contract is concerned with subsidiary rights. If the show plays for twenty-one performances in the West End, the producer usually has the option to acquire the world rights to produce the show. This involves a further payment of about £3,000 to each writer (again, a non-returnable advance against future royalties) covering an option period of three years. He also has the option to keep renewing these rights, for similar amounts and periods, for as long as the show runs in the West End. There are complex definitions of territories, types of production, and so on, but basically, wherever it is produced, you would receive some sort of option payment, plus a royalty, on a similar basis to the West End.

The same sort of arrangement applies to the film rights, but this is where the lawyers really get into their stride. However, since it has taken so many years to film *Evita*, it's probably not something you need to worry about. As for recording rights, the producer has the right to negotiate a deal to record the show, because it is his production, but the writers negotiate a royalty direct with the recording company. Once your material has been recorded, you should register with PRS: the Performing Rights Society (the people who sponsor the Vivian Ellis Prize). They collect and distribute royalties that accrue every time the recording is played: on radio or television,

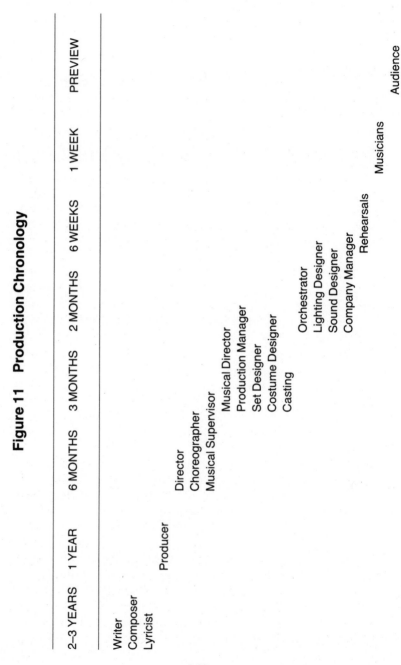

**Figure 11  Production Chronology**

| 2–3 YEARS | 1 YEAR | 6 MONTHS | 3 MONTHS | 2 MONTHS | 6 WEEKS | 1 WEEK | PREVIEW |
|---|---|---|---|---|---|---|---|
| Writer | | | | | | | |
| Composer | | | | | | | |
| Lyricist | | | | | | | |
| | Producer | | | | | | |
| | | Director | | | | | |
| | | Choreographer | | | | | |
| | | Musical Supervisor | | | | | |
| | | | Musical Director | | | | |
| | | | Production Manager | | | | |
| | | | Set Designer | | | | |
| | | | Costume Designer | | | | |
| | | | Casting | | | | |
| | | | | Orchestrator | | | |
| | | | | Lighting Designer | | | |
| | | | | Sound Designer | | | |
| | | | | Company Manager | | | |
| | | | | | Rehearsals | | |
| | | | | | | Musicians | |
| | | | | | | | Audience |

in lifts and shopping malls, or wherever.

## Production chronology

There will be no payment to the writers for any of the production work – meetings, rewrites, auditions, backers' auditions, rehearsals or press calls. The option and royalty advance are all you get at this stage. Travelling expenses and accommodation are provided for the pre-London try-out, but nothing else (except a few lunches and, hopefully, the odd glass of champagne). You will learn so much about writing by taking part in this process, and seeing your work performed to an audience. For a new writer, getting performed is almost more important than getting paid – which, in the current economic climate, is probably just as well.

At this stage it is probably a good idea to plot the progress of the show as it moves towards meeting an audience. Figure 11 shows a rough example of such a chronology.

## The Producer – God bless him

To succeed, producers must possess a unique blend of entrepreneurial, organizational and artistic qualities. They must be able to find money and spend it wisely. More importantly, they must have the vision to see what will be successful, and to control the process by which it is realized. It is an extraordinarily difficult job, which (like other creative people) they don't do for money so much as for the love of the theatre. With perhaps one or two exceptions, producers are not rogues or philistines. They will act in what they perceive to be in the show's best interest, based on their experience.

You have to realize that the Producer has artistic control of the project. He is providing the money which is enabling the production to be staged, and the last word is therefore his. A producer who was particularly fond of a scene which included the arrival and departure of a train, watched patiently as the scene became shorter and shorter during previews. Finally he snapped and said: 'There will be no more cuts in this scene. I've paid good money for that train, and the audience is going to see it.' If the Producer hires Terry Hands to direct a musical biography of George Formby, and Terry sees it as a *Kabuki*-style production, you are not in a position to stop it. You may tactfully draw the producer's attention to the story of the Emperor's new clothes; but if you go around shouting 'I won't have it – this is going to be another *Carrie*!', you'll just be removed from the production. You may be the 'onlie begetter' of the show, but it is vital that you maintain a working relationship with the producer and director – however much (at times) they may seem to have got hold of entirely the wrong end of the stick. If you reach the stage of no longer being on speaking terms with one (or both) of them, your creative influence ceases.

## The creative team

Once the writer's contract is signed, the Producer sets about assembling the creative team and the cast. Generally this starts with the Director, who may have a particular Choreographer, Musical Director or Designer with whom he has worked in the past. Alternatively, the Producer may forge new relationships in the hope of striking a shower of creative sparks. Once complete, it is not unusual for the creative team to have weekend brainstorming sessions, working through the show scene by scene, refining exactly how it will work. You should embrace the opportunity of plundering the experience on offer to you to develop your ideas; the creative team's job is to make it work, but the writers provide the 'it'.

Receiving creative input at the highest level like this should help you to move your work to another plane. Since the original vision is yours, you must make sure that all the team fully understand what that vision is. However, bringing all these creative forces to bear is like an experimental chemical reaction; results can be unpredictable, and a project can strike off at a tangent. Something new is created from the existing elements by the heat of production. Keep your concept, storyline and scene breakdown to hand, and make them, as well as the script, available to all members of the team.

Do not underestimate the importance of the various designers in the realization of your vision. You are creating a world that the audience must believe in. A sympathetic setting can firmly establish this, encouraging the suspension of disbelief, whereas an unsympathetic one can belittle your concept, so that the audience refuses to take your ideas seriously. If the actors are unhappy wearing their costumes (or 'frocks', as they call them), a significant proportion of their energy may be diverted into coping with that, rather than bringing life to your characters – quite apart from the distraction to the audience that outlandish costumes may cause. Bizarre artistic statements are best left for the programme.

It is a strange psychological phenomenon that if the lighting is poor, and people can't see properly, then they can't hear either. This is why farces are usually played in very bright light. Atmospheric lighting is now so popular that the lighting designer may need reminding that he is there to light the actors, not to light the lights; an audience which has difficulty seeing or hearing soon loses interest. The sound department (or 'the noise boys') has the biggest headache. Domestic sound systems now rival those used in shows of a few years ago; the ability to listen has diminished, and each member of the audience imagines they have perfect hearing (generally not true). Adding personal taste to this can produce a situation where someone who thinks it's too loud, and someone who thinks it's too soft can be sitting next to each other.

At this point it may be wise to consider relationships within the production. Figure 12 gives a rough guide to the hierarchy. The Director is the only person with direct access to everyone involved in the production. You must never involve yourself in private arrangements with members of either the cast or creative team without the

## Figure 12    Production Relationships

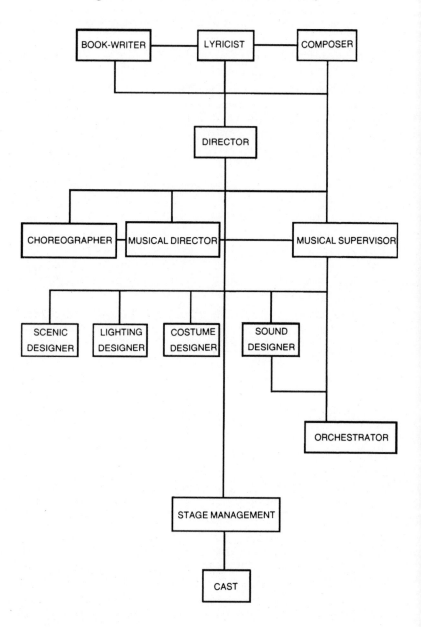

Director's knowledge and acquiescence. The most destructive thing that can happen is for factions to emerge; the director is always right and always has the last word – even when he is wrong. Frank exchanges of views about this must occur only in private.

## Casting

Once the creative team has been put together, casting will take place, and you may be invited to attend. Auditions range widely in scale and tempo. There is the sublime, involving the big names on the producer's 'wish list'. Here the Casting Director sounds out the actor's agent, who says that the actor is interested but will under no circumstances audition. The Casting Director replies that the Director insists that everyone must read. They compromise on a meeting for a chat, at which the Director casually asks the name if he will read. He says, of course he would be happy to.

Then there is the ridiculous: an open dancers' audition announced in *The Stage*. The 500 girls and 200 boys who turn up for ten jobs are given numbers and a card to fill in. The choreographer teaches them a combination, which they do in groups of ten. The numbers of half of them are called out, the rest are dismissed. This goes on until a manageable number remain. These are passed on to the Musical Director; then you find that those who can dance can't sing. This takes all day, and maybe a couple of people are hired. The casting process swings from the depths of depression, when you think the show is uncastable, to the heights of elation, when you finally see someone who *is* the part. All this will stand you in good stead when someone withdraws on the Friday before rehearsals start.

In recent years, because of economic pressures, the size of companies has shrunk. (It is one of the reasons for the exit of the jolly villager.) My first big West End musical was *Showboat*. In those days there were still big casts and a rigid demarcation between singers, dancers and small-part players. The dancers joined in the singing, but weren't expected to produce much noise. The singers would do nothing but stand at the back and sing; any suggestion that they might move, or imbue their contribution with some sort of characterization, was met with a mixture of scorn and contempt. Nowadays, whatever their primary skill, everyone has to be an all-rounder.

Casting can affect the writers in a number of ways, usually detrimentally. Hiring names to improve the bankability of the project may not be in the best interests of the show artistically. Maybe they can't deliver what the part demands, because they lack either the vocal or emotional acting range required; the result is that the score or the book has to be changed. Secondly, a name may overwhelm the part. *Kiss of the Spider Woman* must first and foremost be about the relationship of the two men in the prison cell – Molina and Valentin. But casting Chita Rivera as the Spider Woman cannot but make it appear to be about her – so the focus of the show is lost. Thirdly, if the leads have sufficient clout, you may be at the mercy of their friends' opinions during previews. The friends may tell them things that are not in the best interests of the show as a whole. My experience includes someone persuading the producer to pay a sitcom-writing friend of theirs a vast sum to come up with twenty jokes to make their part funnier. Fortunately the director refused to put all but one of them into the show.

## The money

While the casting continues, the Producer sets about raising the money to finance all this. Like most producers, he may have regular investors who back all his shows, but – as production costs continue to rise and available money doesn't – he will also be looking for new ones. An Investment Proposal will be circulated to existing and prospective backers. This will include a brief description of what the show is about and how it is to be staged (an expanded version of the concept and the selling copy), biographies of the cast and creative team, and a budget.

Quite often there will be a Backers' Audition. Rather like a showcase, this is an informal gathering at which excerpts from the score will be performed to encourage prospective investors to part with their money. The Producer will describe the show, and the Director will narrate the story, while the leading actors (if they have been cast by that stage) will sing some of the songs. This is usually followed by refreshments, which enables investors to mingle with the actors and creatives. You would normally be expected to attend and take part in this process to help sell the show.

On Broadway, shows are so expensive to mount now, and the money so hard to raise, that the list of producers is often longer than the cast list. If they differ amongst themselves as to the artistic vision, the writers can find themselves in real trouble. Fortunately in London we have not yet reached that stage.

## Rehearsals

The rehearsal period is normally four or five weeks in a studio or church hall, before moving into the theatre. It starts with the first read-through, with the entire cast and creative team present. The director talks about his ideas for the show, and the designers will bring the set model and costume designs to explain how it is to be realized. It is important for everyone to know what they are aiming for, as this is the last time they will all be together for some while.

Usually at least three different rehearsals are conducted simultaneously in different parts of the building, with the company split between them. The Director will work on dialogue scenes, while the Choreographer sets the dancing and the Musical Director teaches the songs. Rehearsals may go on from ten in the morning until seven or eight at night, six days a week.

When you see the scenes on their feet, changes may

need to be made. Writers usually attend some rehearsals, if not all of them, and they are constantly challenged by actors and the Director to justify their characters' lines or actions. You may find actors who are uncomfortable saying certain lines or playing certain scenes. Diplomacy is needed in dealing privately with the Director to establish which of the actor's demands you should give in to, and which you should resist. Be prepared for hand-to-hand combat in certain situations. Don't believe anyone who says that musical theatre is a fine example of selfless team effort for the greatest good. It is a group of highly self-motivated individuals who grudgingly admit that it is in their own best interest to co-operate with others to achieve their personal ends.

Because each show is a one-off or prototype, everything is last-minute. Until you are in rehearsal you won't be able to routine the numbers (work out their final form) deciding the number of verses, length of dance sections, underscoring, introductions and keys. The title number of *Hello Dolly*, probably the greatest show-stopper of all time, could only have been created on the rehearsal room floor; no writer could ever have achieved that simply on the page. Only as you go along will you know how much underscoring or scene-change music you will need. You can change a line or a lyric quite easily, but music has to be orchestrated, copied and rehearsed with the band – all expensive items.

By the end of the third week, you will have progressed to the first run-through. This is when the entire cast comes together for the first time, and attempts to go from the start of the show through to the end, in sequence. This will probably be the most depressing experience of your life; you will seriously doubt if the show can ever work. First run-throughs are always staged on Saturdays (so that the cast can't ring their agents to try and get out of the show, and the creative team have Sunday to come up with salvage plans). All this is just part of the process, so you must keep your nerve and continue to refine your work.

Once you see the characters in the flesh, the qualities which the actors bring to them may inspire you to re-imagine how they are presented. The remainder of the rehearsal period will alternate between fixing what needs to be fixed in writing, acting and staging, and run-throughs to see if the fixes have worked.

All too soon the five weeks is up, and the show is usually in reasonable shape for the final run-through in the rehearsal room. The company and creative team then leave in high end-of-term spirits for a venue 'somewhere in England' for the three-week pre-London season. Enjoy the euphoria of this moment. All too soon you will be in a dress rehearsal, when you come to grips with the physical production, and further changes may be forced upon you by purely practical considerations.

It is at this point that you may find yourself wondering how you got into this position. You watch an actor who lacks the range for your songs, with a costume he can't move in, attempting choreography he can't execute while singing at the same time; and this is happening in a set that takes forever to change, and looks like nothing on earth when it has been changed (like *Martin Guerre*). You seek solace by retiring to one of the bars. There the Musical Director and the Orchestrator are taking the band through the music – but none of the songs sound like yours, and you wonder if they have the right music. Rest assured, once again, that this is all quite normal. By now you look back on those ten-hour days of rehearsals, with the rosy glow of happy memories. Now it's ten in the morning till midnight at the theatre, then back to the hotel to work on rewrites overnight.

## Oh no! It's the audience

Just when you think things can't get worse, the audience arrives – and they don't laugh at anything (except the serious bits). Major revisions may be required, once you have their creative input. You may find that, in spite of all the planning, the audience is impatient for the story to move on, and cuts in scenes and/or numbers are necessary. If it is having difficulty following the plot, additional exposition may be needed. Sometimes a number may not be doing its job properly, and an alternative has to be written (or an old one resurrected). In the pre-London run of *Peg*, the leading lady's entrance never seemed to work properly, and on the penultimate night it was decided to try a number that had been discarded early in the development process. The song had never even been heard by most members of the production team, although the performer knew it. The Orchestrator worked through the night, writing out all the parts himself, and the following lunch-time saw him slotting the sheets into the pads at a hastily arranged band call. The number went in for the matinee and stayed in thereafter.

The pre-London season generally settles down into a pattern. There is a notes and rehearsal session each afternoon, making small changes, trying new ideas, ironing out problems. Then there is the show, where you will the cast to get it right and the audience to respond. Monitor the audience carefully. Is there programme-rustling at the same point each night? If so, something needs attention. Never run for cover in the interval; be brave – always patrol the bars and pay heed to what you overhear. You may hear something that will give you a clue to solving a problem which has been worrying you for months, or you may find it's not a problem after all. Then it's back to the hotel for a creative-team post mortem to set the agenda for the next day.

It is easy for the creative team to get punch-drunk at this stage and think that any change is for the best. This is not always the case. Check the audience questionnaires and see how the ratings are changing. You must hold on to your original concept.

It's not unusual for producers to gamble on a pre-London season without having signed a London theatre. During the run West End theatre-owners may come and check out the potential of the show before offering a deal. You never know who is in the audience, or what tales they may return to London with, which may do your show good or ill. This adds an extra nail-biting pressure to the proceedings. You may reach the end of the run without securing a transfer, in which case the show will have to be put into storage until a theatre becomes available. On the other hand, assuming you already have a London home, then just as you seem to be making some headway – the actors are more confident, the audiences are enjoying it more, and it seems to be working – the season finishes, and you have to start all over again: and this time it's for real.

## London at last

### The Previews

You have to endure a repeat of the dress-rehearsal period, and your confidence that you know the solutions is sapped by the fact that there are now new problems. You will also find that West End audiences (a mixture of jaded metropolitans and bewildered tourists) respond differently from those you have been used to. Each night the director gives the Preview speech: 'We hope there won't be any problems … we will only stop if we have to … I know you're going to have a great evening' in the usual friendly and confident style. (Now you know what real acting is!) Meanwhile you continue a programme of tweaking to attune the show to your long-term market, which will be more informed and less forgiving than previous ones. Eventually, though, you reach a point where these changes have to stop, so that the cast can be confident in what they are doing by the press night. This is called freezing the show. With *Call Me Madam*, this is what prompted the famous remark by Ethel Merman: 'From now on this show is frozen – call me Miss Birdseye.'

Preview periods in London tend to be limited to around ten days or two weeks. In New York they can go on for weeks, and shows can close without officially opening. Sometimes things can get really desperate. *Legs Diamond*, a show about the infamous gangster, is notorious. Confronted by uninterested audiences, the producers suddenly realized that the leading character was an unsympathetic figure and decided that they should remedy this. The show was rejigged to portray him as really a nice guy, forced against his will to become a mobster and killer (!), and to set the seal on this change a new opening number was conceived. A fascinating diary was published in the *New York Times* that charted the seven days of working around the clock that it took to effect the change. The music was orchestrated, copied and rehearsed; the number and dialogue was choreographed and rehearsed with the full company; new scenery was designed, built and installed; new costumes were designed and made; then there was a full dress rehearsal with the orchestra. Finally came the first performance. The cost: $650,000. The producers' verdict: 'Well, we think it is a *bit* better.'

The major difference between London and New York production is in the attitude to personnel. In London, if anyone from the creative team leaves the show it is regarded as the kiss of death. No matter how bad they are, people are 'coped with'; only on two occasions in my professional life have I known anyone to be fired. In New York they look on replacing half the cast and creative team as a normal part of the creative process. The number of people you have fired is almost a virility symbol. If you're still on your first director people think you must have no chance.

## The first night

Finally, ready or not, comes the first night. People deal with this in different ways. If you're not really secure, there has to be a full dress rehearsal in the afternoon, but generally there is just vocal and physical warm-up for the company to loosen the tension. When I worked with director John Dexter he insisted on running the whole show scene by scene – in reverse order. He said it confused the cast sufficiently to make them really concentrate at the performance. You should try to prepare yourself for the fact that the audience will be unlike any other, and that the particular mixture of excitement and terror will never be repeated.

My personal first night Armageddon was when I stage-managed the London production of *Beatlemania*, an American multimedia show about the Beatles. Much of my cueing of the lighting, audio visual, scenery and the performers was taken from film sequences which appeared throughout the show. Because the British film wasn't ready, we started the previews using material from the American production. Finally we were promised the film to rehearse with on the afternoon of the first night. We were all there, but there was still no film. The show was scheduled to start at seven o'clock. At five past seven the film arrived and was put on the projectors. At seven-fifteen we started the show without any of us knowing what it contained. We did the show, and we got away with it. How? I don't know – as they say, sometimes the magic works, and sometimes it doesn't; that night it did.

### ... and beyond

After the first night you reach the final frontier – the notices. Sadly, few reviews are now published the morning after. You are denied the equivalent of the party at Sardi's when someone walks in with the crits. It also means you are spared people slinking off into the night when the reviews are stinkers. Don't believe anyone who says they don't read the critics. As I have said before, a theatrical performance is not complete without an audience – and critics are generally the most informed audience you will have, so you should certainly listen and take seriously what they say. However, you are not obliged to agree with them, or take any action as a result. Unfortunately, there is currently no critic whose knowledge and experience of musicals equals that of Mark Steyn. Nevertheless, the critics generally understand what makes good theatre, and they can articulate why a show does or doesn't work.

Traditionally, the cast album was recorded on the first

Sunday after opening and rushed into the shops a week later. This meant that the cast, having worked day and night, and suffered the strain of the opening, had to give up their first day off in weeks. Often with their voices shot to pieces, they were expected make a definitive recording in about two takes. Nowadays record companies have to be convinced the show is a hit before contemplating a recording, so it usually occurs some weeks later, with a reasonable amount of studio time.

Most good directors don't abandon productions after the first night, even though one company did write a letter to the *Times* trying to contact theirs (it was Trevor Nunn). They come in from time to time to make sure the show remains fresh. Assuming the show runs, considered changes may be incorporated during cast changes, so that the show can be kept in line with other (usually American) productions.

To sum up, people generally think Mel Brooks' film *The Producers* is a broad comedy. I *know* it is a fly-on-the-wall documentary.

# 9 Presentation of Scripts

## The Parcel from Hell

Second post at the office of Shoestring Productions, and the weary postperson has just trudged up four floors with an armful of unsolicited scripts, plus a few bills. Top of the pile is a large brown re-used and re-addressed envelope torn, tatty and bearing insufficient postage. Inside is a script and a tape (unlabelled), which falls through a hole in the envelope and is separated forever from its show. The script weighs enough to guarantee wrist strain for the reader. It has no information on the outside except for the title of the show and a coffee stain. Inside, it has no introduction and is closely typed on flimsy paper with many illegible hand-written amendments and grammatical and spelling errors. As the pages are turned, out plops a letter, dated April 1989, which begins, 'Dear Mr Mackintosh, I am sending you the script of my new musical …'. The letter is typed on both sides of the paper. There is no return envelope or postage, and the name and address of the author is nowhere prominent.

Just as well. The bulging waste bin beckons invitingly.

Let's hope you don't recognize any of this from your recent submissions to producers. You normally only get one chance to submit your work to any producer, so it needs to look as good as possible. No frail, used envelopes, then, and no outdated or heavily amended scripts. Reading a musical script is a skilled job; and not all producers (or their secretaries) have those skills. You can make the process easier for them by preparing your work professionally. It's best to start by sending the producer a treatment, but you must have a properly laid out script ready. Here's a check list:

1. Good clean up-to-date copy of the script, neatly laid out and printed in a clear typeface on quality paper.
2. Full information on the title page detailing:
   authors (in billing order)
   copyright-holder and/or agent
   contact address and number
   date and version of the script.
3. Clear information about the show, consisting of:
   Synopsis or introduction
   List of characters with description (specifying whether in order of appearance or importance)
   List of scenes and musical numbers (specifying who sings them)
4. Short, clearly labelled tape of the songs.
5. Brief letter explaining why you have sent this particular show to this producer.
6. Return postage and envelope, if you want your material back.

Figure 13 shows sample layouts for items 2 and 3.

If your show is truly a work of genius, you may be able to ignore some or all of the above, but in general, you need all the help you can get at this stage to sell it. Quality of presentation and professional layout of your musical cannot detract from good material – and we all know that a bad script, poorly presented, is so easy to throw into the bin.

It's useful to think about layout and presentation early on. It can help to focus your ideas and enables you to tackle difficult questions head-on. (For example, what is the billing order, who owns the copyright?)

**Figure 13   Sample of information that should accompany a script**

# SING THAT SONG

a new musical on an old nursery rhyme

Music by Arthur Brown
Lyrics by Freda Smith
Book by Joan Green

© 1996 Final Draft
ABC Representation
150 Regent Place
London W1
0171 123 4567

SING THAT SONG

## **LIST OF CHARACTERS**

(in order of importance)

| | |
|---|---|
| King Charlie | a merry old soul |
| Step-Queen Camilla | his second wife |
| Hettie, the maid | a cruelly put upon waif |
| Jack, the cook | a player of knavish tricks |
| Dr Miller | the King's physician |
| Courtiers, common folk, animal-rights activists, the media | |

ii

SING THAT SONG

## SYNOPSIS

There is a great celebration at the palace. The chef has cooked a great pie. When it is opened at the banquet, twenty four blackbirds fly out and they have to order a pizza. Later, the King is doing his accounts, while the Queen's in the parlour having tea. There is a sudden scream from the kitchen garden. In rushes the maid clutching her nose...

## STYLE

This is a parable of modern-day royal life told within the framework of a nursery rhyme.

## PROPOSED SCENIC CONCEPT

The design should reflect a children's story-book, cartoon style. When the audience enters, upstage is a giant book. At the start of the show, the book opens to reveal the main scenic item for the first scene. Further pages are turned for subsequent scenes.

iii

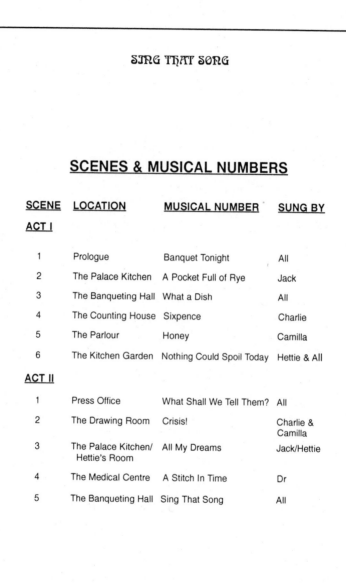

SJNG TRAT SONG

## SCENES & MUSICAL NUMBERS

| SCENE | LOCATION | MUSICAL NUMBER | SUNG BY |
|-------|----------|----------------|---------|
| **ACT I** | | | |
| 1 | Prologue | Banquet Tonight | All |
| 2 | The Palace Kitchen | A Pocket Full of Rye | Jack |
| 3 | The Banqueting Hall | What a Dish | All |
| 4 | The Counting House | Sixpence | Charlie |
| 5 | The Parlour | Honey | Camilla |
| 6 | The Kitchen Garden | Nothing Could Spoil Today | Hettie & All |
| **ACT II** | | | |
| 1 | Press Office | What Shall We Tell Them? | All |
| 2 | The Drawing Room | Crisis! | Charlie & Camilla |
| 3 | The Palace Kitchen/ Hettie's Room | All My Dreams | Jack/Hettie |
| 4 | The Medical Centre | A Stitch In Time | Dr |
| 5 | The Banqueting Hall | Sing That Song | All |

iv

## Page layout

Scripts should be printed on one side of the paper only. The main body should be laid out on the following lines. (See Figure 14 for a practical illustration).

*Headers and/or Footers*, should be included. These are the text at the top and/or bottom of the page, which is repeated on every page (although usually suppressed on title and introductory pages), which can contain page numbering and the date, version and filename.

*Margins, spacing, tabs and indents.* Margins should be approximately 3 cm at top and bottom and left and right, plus any offset required for binding. Single spacing should be used for dialogue and lyrics. Character names should be ranged on the left margin; speech should be indented to the first tab, stage directions to the second.

*Typeface and size.* Standard fonts, such as Times Roman, Arial or Courier are best, because they are clear and universal. Use the 10 or 12 point size (72 points = 1 inch) for proportionally-spaced fonts like Times or Arial, and 10-pitch or 12-pitch for fixed-width (typewriter) fonts like Courier or Elite. Dialogue should be typed in upper and lower case. Lyrics are conventionally typed in capitals and laid out in metrical lines; verses and choruses should be separated by double spacing. Character names and song titles should be in capital letters.

*Numbering.* Traditionally acts are numbered in Roman numerals (I, II, III, IV ...) and scenes and pages in Arabic numerals (1, 2, 3, 4 ...). Each act should start from page one. For easy accessibility, pages should be numbered by act, scene and page thus: I – 2 – 34.

*Scene Headings.* Start a new page for each scene. List the Act, Scene number, time and location.

## Grammar and emphasis

In all dialogue, start each sentence with a capital letter and end with punctuation of some sort. Don't use quotation marks, unless the character is quoting. Obey basic

## Figure 14    Sample of Script Layout

**ACT II SCENE 3**    <u>**ON THE DECK OF THE TITANIC**</u>

It is night. RUBY, in evening dress, stands silhouetted by the deck rail. From below we hear sounds of the party continuing. Enter SAM, coat tails flapping and bow-tie askew.

RUBY      Sam, do you really think she'll go down?

SAM      I guess so Ruby.

RUBY      So this is it. You know I've really enjoyed these last few days.

SAM      So have I. (He kisses her)

RUBY      Make the most of it, Sam. We may not be together much longer.

SAM      Ruby, ever since I met you, you've been telling me that. How come you're still here?

RUBY      You think I'm going to die at a time like this?

SAM      You know, we may be having our ups and downs on this cruise, but it still beats taking the rap for murder.

RUBY      Sam, there's something I've always wanted to ask you. Why did you do it?

SAM      Do what?

RUBY      Murder your wife.

SAM      I don't know. She gave me twenty years of hell. One night, something just snapped. It was her neck.

RUBY      I know how you feel. Many's the time I could have taken an ice pick to Luther.

MSD©30/4/96

| | |
|---|---|
| SAM | Luther? |
| RUBY | My ex. He's an ice man. |
| SAM | Then why did you divorce him? |
| RUBY | No. An Ice Man. He delivers ice all over the world. He tows icebergs from the Antarctic to the Sahara Dessert. |
| SAM | (Correcting her) Sahara Desert. |
| RUBY | No, the Sahara Dessert. It's a night-club in Bermuda. |
| SAM | Ruby, I've decided, if we ever get out of this mess, I'm going to give myself up. I might only get twenty years. Would you wait for me? |
| RUBY | I should live so long. But it's sweet of you to ask. Since I met you, Sam, dying don't seem half so bad. |

<u>SWANSONG</u>

RUBY      THE VOYAGE OF LIFE AIN'T NO PLAIN SAILING
THE SHIP OF FATE CAN CUT UP ROUGH
BUT EVEN THOUGH THE GOING'S TOUGH
I NEVER GET SO MAD I SAY I'VE HAD ENOUGH

'COS PESSIMISM AIN'T MY FAILING
I'M JUST PRAGMATIC I SUPPOSE
SOME TIMES ARE BAD, BUT HEAVEN KNOWS
YOU GOTTA LEARN TO SAY
"THAT'S JUST THE WAY IT GOES"

BUT THIS AIN'T NO WAN SONG
I'M GOING TO CELEBRATE MY GLORIOUS SWANSONG
SO MAYBE THIS OLD GIRL IS DYING
YOU'RE NOT ABOUT TO HEAR ME CRYING

MSD©30/4/96

RUBY    I MAY BE TIRED, I MAY BE AILING
NOT MANY VITAL MOMENTS LEFT
BUT I WILL NEVER BE BEREFT
FOR EVEN WHEN I'M DEAD AND GONE
MY SWANSONG WILL BE LINGERING
ON AND ON, AND ON, AND ON, AND ON AND
ON AND ON, AND ON, AND ON, AND ON AND
ON AND ON, AND ON, AND ON, AND ON AND ON

    A giant wave engulfs RUBY and SAM.
Blackout.

MSD©30/4/96

grammatical conventions unless to do so would be out of character, and try to avoid contentious words or phrases – like 'media' (is it singular or plural nowadays?) – unless you want to make a point, or to collect letters from old colonels by the dozen. Above all, respect the character's voice – if he would split the occasional infinitive, why shouldn't you? But be wary of accents (and particularly of writing them phonetically – this drives everyone crazy); leave that to the actors.

Underlining, **emboldening**, *italicizing*, exclamation marks!!! and CAPITAL LETTERS can all be used to good effect in letters to recalcitrant children and old codgers, but they should be used sparingly in dialogue, or you will irritate the reader and drive the actor insane. Using capitals to make your point is like shouting. IT'S RUDE!!!

I'd just like to say … that an ellipsis (that's three dots) is a pause used when the speech tails off, or concludes without a formal ending. An ellipsis indicates that something has been left unsaid (and, in dialogue, what's not said is often as effective as what is). A dash (—), on the other hand, indicates a break in thought or an interruption.

## Which way is up?

Stage directions are confusing. All stage directions are written from the actor's point of view. 'Stage left' is the *actor's* left when he is facing the audience. 'Up' is upstage, so actors and scenery move **upstage** to move away from the audience and **downstage** to move closer. Scenery (and sometimes actors) go **out** when they fly up in the air, and come **in** when they fly down towards the stage. When a piece of scenery (or a flying actor) is in view it is **in**. When it's raised up out of sight above the proscenium arch (if there is one) it is **out**. **Off** is going away from centre stage towards or into the wings. (Alternatively **off** is what you are when you have missed your entrance.) Don't even think about **prompt** and **OP** – leave that to the techies – but, if you're lucky enough to be out front with the toffs, you

## Figure 15   Stage Plan

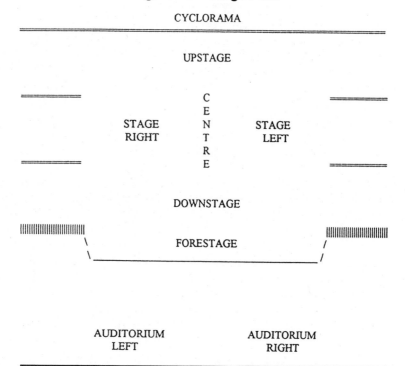

CYCLORAMA

UPSTAGE

STAGE
RIGHT

C
E
N
T
R
E

STAGE
LEFT

DOWNSTAGE

FORESTAGE

AUDITORIUM
LEFT

AUDITORIUM
RIGHT

might just talk about **auditorium left** and **right**. For a diagram, see Figure 15.

Stage directions, aside from the geographical, are the author's method of conveying unspoken events to the actor and thus (hopefully) to the audience. They can be copious (Shaw: 7 pages) or absent (Pinter). Be economical, and treat everyone with reasonable intelligence. Work like a radio play. Try to get the action in the dialogue, and if you can't think of an ending to the scene, don't go for another explosion!

## Hot from the press

*Twang* (a musical about Robin Hood) was the super-flop that brought Lionel Bart's career to a temporary halt in the late 1960s. It was directed by Joan Littlewood, whose working method was to allow the actors to improvise. Shorthand typists in the auditorium took down the dialogue; they delivered it to a small army in the circle bar, who typed it on to stencils and duplicated it. By the time they delivered the results of their labours to the stage, the scene had been cut and other work was in progress.

Life has changed in the last thirty years. Along with electric lighting and indoor sanitation, computers have revolutionized our lives. Scripts continue to change daily, if not hourly, so you need a system of marking revisions, and sophisticated word-processors will do this for you. Firstly, you need to date and time-stamp your work when revising. Some writers print revisions or different generations of scripts on different-coloured paper. What you can't do, though, is give actors complete new scripts in rehearsal, if they've marked up the old one (which they will have done by day one). What they need are inserts with logical page layout and numbering. It's a good idea to think modular, so that sections of script can be added or removed where and when necessary.

You may be a two-finger, sit-up-and-beg typewriter man, but sooner or later your precious work will find its way on to a word-processor. Don't imagine your Luddite mentality is going to give you control over your work, once some smart secretary has the only up-to-date copy on her computer, and you don't even know how to turn it on. Unless you want to remain a Luddite, learn how to work it before you get to that overnight rewrite when the secretary's gone home.

### One for luck

Did you hear about the writer who rigorously backed up his work on disk every night? One morning he woke up to find the house had been burgled, and his computer had been stolen, along with the final draft of the script on the hard disk. He was consoled that he at least had a copy on a floppy disk – until he realized that he had left the floppy in the machine, and they'd taken that too.

So, if it's typed, inscribed, embossed or engraved, do not let it out of your sight unless you have at least two copies. Forget about carbon copies (they are unacceptable); get quality photocopies, and make sure the original is clear, legible and in black or dark ink. If your document has been typed on a word-processor keep a clean master on paper, a copy of the file on the hard disk, and another copy on floppy disk *elsewhere*. And, if you really value your time, keep an extra copy for luck.

## Music

Sooner or later you've got to put aside those lead sheets and chord symbols and write out at least a piano accompaniment of the songs. This is not so you can send them off with the script for potential producers to skim through in their offices. Few producers or directors can read music or have pianists on call, and actors (in most cases) prefer to learn show songs from tape.

You need to put down the melodic and harmonic structure of the songs so that the Musical Director and Orchestrator know what you want. You'll also need piano vocals early on for auditions. These should preferably be on A4 paper, for ease of copying. Don't go any further than that in the pre-production stage. Keys will undoubtedly change and underscore, orchestration and incidental musical is best left fluid. Remember not to frighten off potential producers by demanding a 60-piece orchestra early on.

### Tapes

No-one likes half-empty cassettes. Either write shows that are exactly forty-five minutes each half, or buy professional tapes of the appropriate duration. Type or print labels where possible, and type or print the box insert. Make sure that both are clearly identified with name and contact details. Research shows that people buying houses make their decision in the first minute and a half. With a tape, you probably don't get even that long. Your music will either grab the listener, and he'll want to hear more – or it won't. Either way, he's unlikely to be bothered to rewind the tape or take much care of it. So, if you send out returned tapes for a second journey, make sure that you rewind them to the start. Also, knock out the record tab, so that a tape can't be accidentally over-recorded with something else. Demos should only include pianos and voices which are in tune. (That may sound obvious, but – speaking from experience – it clearly isn't obvious to everyone.)

## Give me the tools ...

If you're really serious about this writing business, you need decent tools. Book-writers, lyricists and composers can all use electronics to aid the creative process. Having these resources at your disposal twenty-four hours a day, seven days a week is an enormous leap of empowerment.

First of all, get yourself an up-to-date computer with a professional word-processor, and a quality printer: laser for preference. You can then write, rewrite, adapt, document, file and retrieve your work with the maximum of flexibility, and the minimum of effort.

Add a modem and a simple text scanner, and you'll have fax and Internet connections, plus document-transfer and copying facilities. Then, if you have a new lyric for the composer, or a new scene for the director, it can be with them in seconds. This shows up the process of summoning a single-figure-IQ Hells Angel and trusting him to deliver your precious cargo for the farce that it is. Electronic mail is the fastest and cheapest way of getting your script round the world, via the Internet. Composers can even send sound files this way.

Composers can link music keyboards to a computer

with MIDI (musical instrument digital interface), and appropriate software allows you to input, edit, play back and print music of any complexity, easily and without expert knowledge. This is to music what advanced word-processing is to text. Mechanical tasks, such as editing, repeating music, transposing and extracting parts, are simple. You can play (with one finger), record and print out the orchestrations.

But paper won't be dead until actors can hold electronic scripts in their hands. Whatever paper you choose – vellum, parchment, whatever – avoid something that is so thin that you can see through it. Go for, say, A4 white bond of 70–100 gm weight. Scripts in permanent glitzy bindings look good for producers. They are no good for updates, though and so are useless for actors; loose binding is best for this purpose.

## The postcard test

Producers aren't looking for scripts – they're looking for ideas. You should be able to write a brief description of your musical on a plain postcard – a combination of the concept and the selling copy. Do this at the outset and repeat it frequently as the show develops. It will help to focus on the key points, and keep your mind on your original intentions.

People are always terrified that someone will steal their idea. Well, there's no copyright in ideas, but your idea is special to you. The way you handle it is what's unique about it, what makes it your concept.

So write that postcard and address it to the producer of your choice. If you don't get a favourable response, maybe they don't like the idea, why send them the script?

(And, no, it doesn't have to be a postcard. An electronic mail message, a fax, a phone call or sky-writing will serve the same function, as long as you keep it brief. Brevity is the soul of ...)

# 10 The Future of the Musical

The short answer to the question 'Whither the musical?' is 'Beats me guv'. The current position is that fewer and fewer producers are presenting bigger and bigger shows that cost more and more. They therefore have to be safer and safer bets, and so come from fewer and fewer writers. This cannot be in the long-term interest of musical theatre.

## The mega-musicals

The problem with mega-musicals is that they are like dinosaurs: too big to be sustainable. When I first started in the theatre you could put on a modest play in a medium-sized house, at reasonable seat prices, and recoup the cost of production in six weeks, and six months or a year was a highly successful run. This encouraged people to take a chance on what they produced, because the odds were reasonable. Few of the great classic musicals, which we think of as smash hits, ran for more than fifteen months in their original productions; that was the standard length of contracts at the time.

Now shows find it difficult to recoup within a year, and so they have to be geared to global marketing. We define smash hits as running for ten years. The result is that these long-running shows are clogging up theatres and starving the West End of opportunities to present new work. They are also pushing seat prices up to a point at which new audiences are deterred. It is common now to see only a very small difference between top and bottom prices, and one price in each level of the theatre. More importantly, the long-running shows are often not as interesting or success-ful artistically as other shows that have come and gone. Could anyone actually say that *Miss Saigon* (the longest-running show in the history of the Theatre Royal Drury Lane) deserved the title of the best? Best-marketed perhaps.

This expense is self-defeating. We can't afford to produce on this scale any more. Even Andrew Lloyd Webber, talking about the transmogrification of *Jeeves* into the simpler *By Jeeves*, has admitted as much. There are no more big theatres left to produce big shows in – they are all housing long runners. We need to be looking at more modest shows that can be successfully staged in medium sized venues for reasonable runs; is there nothing to be learned from the fact that the longest-running musical of all time is *The Fantasticks*, which employs minimal resources? Quality of writing needs to be the criterion – not suitability for worldwide marketing. On this smaller scale, new musical writing can be more viable, although there is the snobbery against musicals occupying smaller theatres which some people would like to see reserved specifically for plays (regardless of their quality).

High costs and poor returns have discouraged new producers from starting up, and existing producers from taking a chance on new writers. A vicious circle has been created. The only people willing to finance new work seem to be loony millionaires, who fancy dabbling in theatre, but have no artistic judgement, and so fund hopeless projects that crash spectacularly. Thus the quotable odds against success for new work are pushed up even further and regular investors frightened off.

## New writing

Meanwhile, there is a great deal of new writing talent around, but it is not getting produced. I attend many workshops and showcases, and I see some excellent work, but it rarely moves on to full-scale production. No one is prepared to put up the money to allow these new writers to be seen. The companies who are making substantial returns from current successes are not investing in the future as they should; they are receiving huge profits, but are not ploughing anything back – their moral duty is not being discharged. True, there is the Mackintosh Foundation and a small amount of good works by Really Useful Group, but just one percent of total theatrical profits invested directly in new writing would transform the situation.

Note, though, that I'm not talking about handouts; I mean investment with a view to further profits. Any portfolio of quality new shows should provide a return on some of them. If these companies don't want to take on the work of administering the funds or producing the shows themselves, there are plenty of people who would be happy to do it. What musical theatre really needs is something like the National Film Finance Board to support new work by topping up production budgets to allow it to be produced. As Dolly Levi once famously remarked: 'Money is like manure. Ya gotta spread it around to help small things grow.'

There is a crisis in new play-writing, too, but this is because new writers are choosing to work in television, because of the bigger demand for product and the greater financial rewards. Many recent, highly praised new theatre plays have not been worthy of the well-intentioned hype, and have not attracted an audience.

## The venues

London lacks the infrastructure to support and develop new writers that New York has. On Broadway, it is even more difficult to get new work performed than in London. Off Broadway, however, there is a whole tier of houses teeming with talent and opportunity to bring on new writing. Even established writers are now launching new work in this environment. Unfortunately in London there is just one venue (the Donmar Warehouse) that is comparable to an off-Broadway house. Our fringe venues are mostly so decrepit that they would barely count as off-off-Broadway. We need more well-run, properly equipped, comfortable, centrally located, small venues for new work to be seen in – and finance for shows to be put on in them. Writers and shows could then move from there to reinvigorate West End theatre. National Lottery money seems to be available for opera (even though it stirs up protest), because it is somehow deemed more worthy, even though, as Geoffrey Smith said: 'Opera is the theatre of the absurd, set to music'. Therefore, because of snobbery, musical theatre (though equally valid in artistic terms) is ignored.

It is encouraging that subsidized theatres are producing musicals, though only because they see them as a way of boosting attendances. Unfortunately, musicals are sometimes regarded as a soft option for bringing in money to subsidize the 'real work' of staging plays; this usually means that the older big-name shows are revived, because they are seen as having an established audience. Such theatres don't have the same commitment to staging new musical work as they have to staging new plays. Audiences are seen as compartmentalized into 'real playgoers' (who wouldn't go to a musical) and people who 'just come to musicals'. In fact much new musical writing explores current issues and experiments with new forms – which is exactly the sort of thing that is suited to the playgoing audience. If theatres had the vision to include musicals in their commitment to new writing, and if they promoted them in the same way, they might be pleasantly surprised by the results, both artistically and financially.

## What kind of shows?

As to defining the future for the medium itself, the history of musical theatre has generally been one of evolution, rather than revolution. There has been a slow move towards more music, with more complex scores and greater integration of the numbers. The overall quality of the writing of both book and lyrics has steadily risen. Shows have tackled progressively more serious subjects, and the term 'musical play' is succeeding the term 'musical comedy'. (The term has been around longer than you might think, though – *Oklahoma!* was described as a musical play.)

Most of the landmark shows (*Hair, Jesus Christ Superstar, A Chorus Line, Cats, They're Playing Our Song*), hailed as changing the history of the musical irrevocably, in the end proved to be one-off events. They just nudged things forward a little. By and large, rock music has made little impact in the theatre; it has simply been absorbed and digested.

For all that Boublil and Schonberg have been hailed as new and radical, they are actually the opposite. Their histrionic style is a return to 'hiss the villain' melodrama, quite at odds with the increasingly naturalistic style of others. They are producing work in an operatic non-realistic tradition.

Perhaps the future lies in tackling more and more subjects that have hitherto been deemed not suitable for a musical. Surely we can finally throw off the idea that music somehow trivializes its subject matter. The future may lie in the convergence of musical theatre and opera that people have been predicting for some time. On the other hand, it may involve a return to a greater reliance on dialogue, which will make the songs more special. Maybe contemporary subjects will finally come into their own.

Most likely something unexpected will happen. Wherever the future of the musical lies, and whatever it contains, it will not come from Andrew Lloyd Webber, Boublil and Schonberg, or even Stephen Sondheim. And it will certainly not come from the Disney Organization moving its entire catalogue from screen to stage. It will be new, and it will come from a completely unexpected quarter. Maybe, after you have read this book, it will come from you.

# Resources

## Bibliography

Bell, Marty, *Backstage On Broadway* (Nick Hern Books, London, 1994)

Bergreen, Laurence, *As Thousands Cheer: The Life of Irving Berlin* (Hodder & Stoughton, London, 1990)

Billington, Michael, *Performing Arts* (QED, London, 1980)

Bordman, Gerald, *American Musical Theatre* (Oxford University Press, New York, 1986)

Brahms, Caryl, and Ned Sherrin, *Song By Song: 14 Great Lyric Writers* (Ross Anderson, Bolton, 1984)

Citron, Stephen, *The Musical from The Inside Out* (Hodder & Stoughton, London, 1991)

— *The Wordsmiths: Oscar Hammerstein 2nd & Alan Jay Lerner* (Sinclair-Stevenson, London, 1996)

Engel, Lehman, *The Making of a Musical* (Harper & Row, New York, 1986)

— *Words And Music* (Schirmer, New York, 1981)

Fordin, Hugh, *Getting To Know Him* (Da Capo, New York, 1995)

Frankel, Aaron, *Writing The Broadway Musical* (Drama Book Publishers, New York, 1991)

Ganzl, Kurt, *Musicals* (Carlton Books, London, 1995)

— *Ganzl's Book Of The Broadway Musical* (Schirmer, New York, 1995)

Ganzl, Kurt, and Andrew Lamb, *Ganzl's Book Of The Musical Theatre* (Bodley Head, London, 1988)

Gelbart, Larry, David Zipple and Cy Coelman, *City of Angels: Libretto* (Applause, New York, 1990)

Gottfried, Martin, *Broadway Musicals* (Abradale/Abrams, New York, 1979)

— *More Broadway Musicals: Since 1980* (Abradale/Abrams, New York, 1991)

— *Opening Nights* (G P Putnam's Sons, New York, 1969)

Gray, Simon, *An Unnatural Pursuit* (Faber & Faber, London, 1985)

Green, Benny, *A Hymn To Him: The Lyrics Of Alan Jay Lerner* (Pavilion, London, 1987)

Green, Stanley, *The Encylopedia Of Musical Theatre* (Da Capo, New York, 1984)

— *The Rodgers and Hammerstein Story* (Da Capo, New York, 1963)

— *The World Of Musical Comedy* (Da Capo, New York, 1990)

Hart, Moss, *Act One* (Hodder & Stoughton, London, 1987)

Hirsch, Foster, *Harold Prince And The American Musical Theatre* (Cambridge University Press, 1989)

Hirschfeld, Al, *Show Business Is No Business* (Da Capo, New York, 1979)

Hischak, Thomas S., *Word Crazy* (Praeger, New York, 1991)

Jackson, Arthur, *The Book Of Musicals* (Webb & Bower, London, 1977)

Kasha, Al, and Joel Hirschhorn, *Notes On Broadway* (Contemporary Books, Chicago, 1985)

Kislan, Richard, *The Musical: A Look At The American Musical Theatre* (Prentice-Hall, Englewood Cliffs, 1980)

Lerner, Alan Jay, *The Street Where I Live* (Columbus, London, 1989)

Mordden, Ethan, *Broadway Babies* (Oxford University Press, New York, 1983)

Mamet, David, *Writing In Restaurants* (Faber & Faber, London, 1988)

Mandelbaum, Ken, *Not Since Carrie* (St Martin's Press, New York, 1991)

Marsolas, Ken, Rodger McFarlane and Tom Viola, *Broadway Day and Night: Backstage and Behind The Scenes* (Packet Books, New York, 1992)

Nelson, Richard and David Jones, *Making Plays: The*

*Writer/Director Relationship In The Theatre Today* (Faber & Faber, London, 1995)

Nolan, Frederick, *Lorenz Hart: A Poet On Broadway* (Oxford University Press, New York, 1994)

Rogers, Richard, *Musical Stages* (Da Capo, New York, 1995)

Sherrin, Ned, *Ned Sherrin's Theatrical Anecdotes* (Virgin, London, 1991)

— *Ned Sherrin in his Anecdotage,* (Virgin, London, 1993)

Simon, Neil, Marvin Hamlisch and Carol Bayer Sager, *They're Playing Our Song: Libretto* (Random House, New York, 1980)

Steyn, Mark, 'Adapting To Survive', *Drama Magazine,* 1988, vol. 4

— 'The Modern Musical', *Drama Magazine,* 1989, vol. 3

Swain, Joseph P., *The Broadway Musical: A Critical And Musical Survey* (New York, Oxford University Press, 1990)

Young, David, *How To Direct A Musical (Broadway Your Way)* (Routledge, New York, 1995)

Zadan, Craig, *Sondheim & Co* (Pavilion, London, 1987)

## Reference works and trade directories

*The Arc Musicians' Directory* (Arc Publishing, London, 1994)

*The British & International Music Yearbook* (Rhinegold, London, annual)

*The British Theatre Directory* (Richmond House, London, biennial)

Sharman, Helen, *Bums On Seats: How To Publicise Your Show* (A & C Black, London, 1992)

*Contacts* (The Spotlight, London, annual)

Bender, Hy, *Essential Software For Writers* (Writers Digest Books, Cincinnati, 1994)

Sleath, Julian, *Fringe Safety* (Edinburgh Festival Fringe Society, 1995)

Billington, Michael, *Guinness Book Of Theatre Facts And Feats* (Guinness, London, 1982)

Larkin, Colin, *Guinness Who's Who Of Stage Musicals*

(Guinness, London, 1994)

*How To Do A Show On The Fringe* (Edinburgh Festival Fringe Society, 1995)

Buchanan, Stuart, *How To Sell A Show On The Fringe* (Edinburgh Festival Fringe Society, 1995)

Baskerville, David, *The Music Business Handbook* (Sage Publications, Thousand Oaks, 1995)

Winslow, Colin, *The Oberon Glossary Of Theatrical Terms (Theatre Jargon Explained)* (Oberon Books, London, 1991)

Heywood, Brian and Roger Evan, *The PC Music Handbook* (PC Publishing, London, 1996)

*The Penguin Dictionary For Writers And Editors* (Viking, London, 1994)

*Theatre Guide* (Formerly The British Alternative Theatre Directory) (Rebecca Books, London, biennial)

*The White Book*
  (Birdhurst, London, annual)

*The Writers' And Artists' Year Book* (A & C Black, London, annual)

Kenyon, Sherrilyn, with Hal Blythe and Charlie Sweet, *The Writers Digest Character-Naming Sourcebook* (Writers Digest, Cincinnati, 1994)

*The Writer's Companion* (Macmillan, London, 1996)

*The Writer's Handbook* (Macmillan, London, annual)


## Journals

*Amateur Stage*
Platform Publications
83 George Street, London, W1H 5PL
0171 486 1732    Fax: 0171 224 2215


*London Theatre Record*
4 Cross Deep Gardens, Twickenham, TW1 4QU
0181 893 6087


*Musical Stages*
PO Box 8365, London, W14 0GL
Phone/Fax: 0171 603 2221

*PCR: Production & Casting Report*
PO Box 100, Broadstairs, Kent, CT10 1UJ
01843 860885

*Plays & Players*
Northway House, 1379 High Road, London N20 9LP
0181 343 8515

*The Stage*
47 Bermondsey Street, London, SE1 3XT
0171 403 1818    Fax: 0171 403 1418

*Theatre*
Repertory Publishing
PO Box 7913, London, SE1 4EZ
0171 378 1069

*Variety*
34 Newman Street, London, W1P 3PD
0171 637 3663

*Writers News*
PO Box 4, Nairn, IV12 4HU
01667 54441    Fax: 01667 54401

## Useful organizations

Barbican Centre Library (music database)
Silk Street, London, EC2Y 8BQ
0171 638 0569

BASCA (British Academy of Songwriters, Composers & Authors)
34 Hanway Street, London, W1P 9DE
0171 436 2261

British Library
Great Russell Street, London, WC1 3DG
0171 636 1544

Directors Guild of Great Britain
15 Great Titchfield Street, London, W1P 7FB
0171 436 8626    Fax: 0171 436 8646

Edinburgh Festival Fringe Society
180 High Street, Edinburgh, EH1 1QS
0131 226 5257    Fax: 0131 220 4205
E-mail: admin@edfringe.org.uk

FACADE (courses, readers reports, workshops)
43A Garthorne Road, London, SE23 1EP
0181 699 8655

Fringe Theatre Network (theatre listing/availability)
72 Landor Road, London, SW9 9PH
0171 737 5943

The Mercury Workshop
Suite 51, 26 Charing Cross Road, London, WC2H 0DH
0171 240 2009

New Playwright's Trust
The Interchange Studios, Dalby Street, London, NW5 3NO
0171 284 2818

Performing Rights Society (Vivian Ellis Prize)
29–33 Berners Street, London, W1P 4AA
0171 580 5544 ext 8310

Playwrights Co-operative
61 Collier Street, London, N1 9BE
0171 713 7125

*The Spotlight* (Directory)
7 Leicester Place, London, WC2H 7BP
0171 437 7631    Fax: 0171 437 5881

The Theatre Museum (British Theatre Association Library)
1E Tavistock Street, London, WC2E 7PA
0171 836 7891

Theatre Writers Union
The Actor's Centre, 1B Tower Street, London, WC2H 9NP
0181 883 7520

Writers Guild Of Great Britain
430 Edgware Road, London, W2 1EH
0171 723 8074

## Courses and workshops

The Arvon Foundation (playwriting/scriptwriting)
Lumb Bank, Heptonstall, Hebden Bridge, West Yorkshire, HX7 6DF
01422 843714

FACADE
See preceding section

London Screenwriters Workshop
84 Wardour Street, London, W1V 3LF
0171 434 0492

## Competitions

Musical Of The Year (biennial)
Danmarks Radio TV-Provinsfdelingen
Olof Palmes Alle 10–12, DK-8200, Aarhus N, Denmark.
0045 87 39 71 11   Fax: 0045 87 39 71 04

Vivian Ellis Prize (annual)
Performing Rights Society
See under Useful Organizations above.

## Music software

*Cubase Score*
(Steinberg)
Harmon Audio
Unit 2, Boreham Wood Industrial Estate, Rowley Lane, Boreham Wood, WD6 5PZ
0181 207 5050
Internet: http://www.steinberg-us.com

*Encore*
(Passport)
Arbiter Group
Balkanar House, Wilberforce Road, London NW9
0181 202 1199

*Finale*
(Coda Music Technology)
MCM, 9 Hatton Street, London, NW8 8PR
0171 723 7221

*Sibelius 7*
Sibelius Software, 75 Burleigh Street, Cambridge, CB1 1DJ
01223 302765    Fax: 01223 351947
e-mail: sales@sibelius.demon.co.uk
Internet: http://www.acorn.co.uk/developers/sibelius/

## Suppliers and retailers

Argent Zwemmer Printed Music (mail-order service available)
20 Denmark Street, London, WC2H 8NA
0171 379 3384    Fax: 0171 379 3398

Chappell of Bond Street (music sales and publishers)
50 New Bond Street, London, W1V 9HA
0171 491 2777    Fax: 0171 491 0133

Dress Circle (show records, music and books; mail-order service available)
57–59 Monmouth Street, Upper St Martin's Lane, London, WC2H 9DG
0171 240 2227   Fax: 0171 379 8540
Internet: http://www.dresscircle.co.uk

First Night Records
2 Fitzroy Mews, London, W1P 5DQ
0171 383 7767

French's Theatre Book Shop (mail-order service available)
52 Fitzroy Street, London, W1P 6JR
0171 387 9373

Offstage Theatre Bookshop (new and second-hand)
37 Chalk Farm Road, London NW1 8AJ
0171 485 4996

Panache Partnership (tapes: blank and duplication)
16 Elm Road, Brixham, Devon, TQ5 0DH
01803 8544744

Rare Discs
18 Bloomsbury Street, London, WC1B 3QA
0171 580 3516

Royal National Theatre Bookshop
Upper Ground, London, SE1 9PX
0171 633 0880

Soho Soundhouse/Turnkey (computer music applications)
114–116 Charing Cross Road, London, WC2H 0DT
0171 379 5148   Fax: 0171 379 0093

Stanley Productions (Blank Tapes)
147 Wardour Street, London, W1V 3TB
0171 439 0311   Fax: 0171 434 0592

# The Internet

## *Web Sites*

Directory Of Theatre Professionals On The Net
http://www.theatre-central.com/dir/pro/

Gilbert & Sullivan Archive
http://diamond.idbsu.edu/gas/GaS.html

Internet Stage & Screen Resources
http://www.the-wire.com/stagenet/

Musicals Home Page
http://www.musical.mit.edu/musical/

Musical Theater Stanford
http://www.akebono.stanford.edu/yahoo/entertainment/
music/musicals

Stephen Sondheim Stage
http://www.sondheim.com/

tGP Goldsmith Playlist
http://www.gold.ac.uk/tgp/welcome.htmlgwriting/

Theatre Central
http://www.theatre-central.com/

TheatreNet
http://www.theatrenet.com/

Theatre Resources On The Net
http://www.icam.fr/divers/theatre-e.html

Tower Lyrics Archive
http://www.ccs.neu.edu/home/tower/lyrics.html

UK Theatre Web
http://www.uktw.co.uk/

World Wide Arts Resources
http://concourse.com/wwar/defaultnew.html

Yahoo Theater Directory
http://www.yahoo.com/entertainment/music/
http://www.yahoo.com/entertainment/songwriting/
http://www.yahoo.com/entertainment/theater/arts/drama/
   musicals/

*Mailing Lists*

Musical Mailing List
http://server.berkley.edu/%/eayukawa/lomml.html

*Newsgroups*

http://www.ncook.k12.il.us/cgi-bin/newsgroups

*Usenet Groups*

rec.arts.theatre.musicals
news:misc.writing

# Glossary

**active songs**: Songs that move the plot forward, thus changing the situation.

**anagnorisis**: Putting a character in jeopardy by the disclosure of previously unknown facts.

**arranger**: The person who develops the LEAD SHEETS into the final versions of songs, often responsible for creating linking, underscoring and dance music. This work is now often done by the MUSICAL SUPERVISOR.

**backers' audition**: An event (like a SHOWCASE) staged for prospective investors, to encourage their participation.

**ballads**: Songs that are smooth-flowing and melody-dominant. They are generally reflective.

**book**: The spine that supports the body of the show, whether it has dialogue or whether it is through-written.

**book doctor/script doctor**: Someone from outside the CREATIVE TEAM who contributes to changes to the script of a show during production.

**character background**: A detailed description of a character, together with his background, attitudes and possible dialogue.

**character plot**: A detailed description of a character's attitudes and actions in each scene.

**chest voice**: That part of a performer's vocal register that resonates in the chest. (See HEAD VOICE.)

**chord**: Any combination of three or more notes simultaneously performed.

**comedy/point numbers**: Songs whose main purpose is to be funny, where the lyric is more important than the tune.

**commercial potential**: The reason why an audience would be interested in seeing a show. The reasons which will generate demand by an audience to buy tickets for a show (sought by producers and investors).

**concept**: A sentence or two defining the idea for a show, and how it is to be treated, encapsulating the artistic and commercial potential.

**contractions**: Words in a lyric that are shortened, because there are too many syllables to fit the tune. (See FILLERS.)

**copying**: Writing out (usually by hand) the music from which each member of the orchestra will play.

**counterpoint**: Two different tunes sung at the same time.

189

# Glossary

**creative team**: Those responsible for realizing a production – writers, director, choreographer, musical director and designers.

**demo tape**: A selection of perhaps six varied songs, capturing the flavour of a show, which can be used to promote it.

**deus ex machina**: A dramatic device by which external (originally divine) intervention is used to resolve the plot.

**development**: Adding new and unforeseen twists to the initial situation, putting major characters in joepardy.

**director**: The leader of the creative team.

**dots**: The written music.

**downstage**: At or towards the front of the stage, closest to the audience.

**dramatic shape**: The pattern of events in the story, incorporating exposition, development and resolution.

**dummy lyric**: A temporary lyric, used to demonstrate the number of syllables in each line, the rhyme scheme and lyric form.

**exposition**: Introducing characters and situations to an audience.

**fillers**: Words that have no meaning that are added to a lyric to make it fit the tune. (See CONTRACTIONS.)

**fixer**: The orchestral manager, who engages, organizes and disciplines the musicians.

**foreshadowing/signposting**: planting a fact (in an innocuous way) early in the story that will be needed later in the plot.

**freezing of the show**: The point during production after which no further changes are made.

**harmony**: The simultaneous sounding of different notes in a way that is musically significant.

**head voice**: That part of a performer's vocal register that resonates in the head. (See CHEST VOICE.)

**hook**: A clever musical or lyrical idea which grabs the listener's attention, and which they will remember.

**key**: The defining notes or scales that form the basis of a tune.

**laundry-list songs**: Songs that rely for their effect on clever or witty lists of items.

**lead sheet**: The composer's equivalent of a script, used to convey his intentions.

**melody**: A succession of notes that has a recognizable shape – and should be 'rememberable'.

**metre**: The measured arrangement of syllables (stressed and unstressed, long and short) in a line or phrase.

**modulation**: Lifting the key up by a half-tone. (Whole-tone modulation is also possible.)

**musical director**: The person in charge of the music on a nightly basis and responsible for maintaining standards. In rehearsal the musical director sets keys and teaches the music to the artists; in performance he or she conducts.

**musical play/play with music**: In a musical play, the songs are integral to the story-telling; without them it is incomplete. In a play with music the songs add an extra dimension to a drama that could exist without them.

**musical supervisor**: The head of the music department (often assuming the functions of an ARRANGER), who supervises subsequent productions.

**option**: The right to produce a show for a particular period of time.

**orchestrator**: The person who writes the notes that each individual musician will play, and who is responsible for the overall sound.

**perfect rhyme**: A rhyme in which vowels, consonants and stresses echo each other exactly.

**peripeteia**: Putting a character in jeopardy by a sudden reversal of fortune.

**piano vocal score**: A development of the LEAD SHEET that defines the composer's intentions more precisely.

**play with music**: See MUSICAL PLAY/PLAY WITH MUSIC.

**plot point**: New information that helps to move the story forward.

**pop song**: See SHOW SONGS/POP SONGS.

**post-card test**: An encapsulation of your show in a few sentences.

**producer**: The person ultimately responsible for staging a show: raising the finance, hiring the CREATIVE TEAM and managing its execution and day-to-day running.

**production number**: Full-company numbers that are used to introduce locations or relationships.

**range**: The spectrum of notes over which a singer (or instrument) can produce sounds.

**reader's report**: A professional, written appraisal of a script and tape.

**reading**: When the script is read and sung through out loud in order to gain an indication of how it will work.

**reflective songs**: Songs that tell you something new about a character or situation.

**reprise**: A return to (*not* a repeat of) a song later in the story, which can point up developments in character or plot.

**resolution**: The realistic and satisfying conclusion of a story.

**resolution, point of**: Point in the story where it starts to conclude.

**rhyme**: The identical sounding of entire or parts of words in corresponding positions in a musical phrase.

**rhyme scheme**: The pattern of rhymes within a group of lines forming a section in a song – abcb, aabb, abab

**rhythm**: The defining element of a song, expressed as a time signature: e.g. 2/4, 3/4, 4/4.

**rhythm numbers**: Songs that are rhythm dominant and have a definite sense of movement. They are generally active.

**royalty**: A percentage of the weekly gross box-office takings paid to writers and creative team.

**scène à faire**: A scene that must be included to fulfil the audience expectation that has been created.

**scene breakdown**: The story broken down into specific scenes, detailing location, time, action and characters involved.

**script doctor**: See BOOK DOCTOR.

**selling copy**: A paragraph, amplifying the CONCEPT, which you can use to sell your idea (like material used on a handbill).

**showcase**: A professional presentation of a new work staged in order to sell it.

**show songs/pop songs**: Show songs are more complex and more specific than pop songs. Although the music repeats, the lyrics in each block must be different, and the song idea must be resolved by the end.

**signposting**: See FORESHADOWING.

**song analysis**: A list of songs detailing their location, type, content and who sings them.

**song form**: The arrangement of musical blocks of sections forming a song: AABA, ABAC, ABAB.

**song points**: Those points at which the story will benefit from being told in song rather than in dialogue.

**stage directions**: Method of explaining your intentions, and unspoken events to the actors and creative team.

**story line**: A detailed description of what happens in the story.

**stress**: Whereabouts in a line or phrase the emphasis is placed.

**structure**: How the material is organized and the story is told. A blueprint that incorporates the action, characters and dramatic premise.

**sympathetic characters**: Characters with whom the audience can identify and become emotionally involved.

**syncopation**: The accenting of a beat that is not the main accented beat in a bar.

**tempo**: The speed at which the counts of the rhythm are played.

**theme**: A timeless universal statement about the human condition which can be drawn from the story.

**treatment**: A five-page encapsulation of a show, including CONCEPT, STORYLINE and list of characters.

**through-written**: A show in which dialogue is (virtually) eliminated and everything is sung.

**tutti**: A song, or section of music performed by all voices or instruments.

**underscore**: Music that is played 'under' or 'behind' dialogue.

**unities (of time, place and action)**: Proposition by Aristotle that the plot of a play should be single and should unfold in the course of a single day and in one location.

**upstage**: At or towards the back of the stage, furthest from the audience.

**workshop**: A professional rehearsed and staged reading of a new work.